Linux
Pocket Guide

Linux
Pocket Guide

Daniel J. Barrett

O'REILLY®

Beijing · Cambridge · Farnham · Köln · Paris · Sebastopol · Taipei · Tokyo

Linux Pocket Guide
by Daniel J. Barrett

Copyright © 2004 O'Reilly Media, Inc. All rights reserved.
Printed in the United States of America.

Published by O'Reilly Media, Inc., 1005 Gravenstein Highway North,
Sebastopol, CA 95472.

O'Reilly Media, Inc. books may be purchased for educational, business, or
sales promotional use. Online editions are also available for most titles
(*safari.oreilly.com*). For more information, contact our corporate/
institutional sales department: (800) 998-9938 or *corporate@oreilly.com*.

Editor:	Mike Loukides
Production Editor:	Colleen Gorman
Cover Designer:	Emma Colby
Interior Designer:	David Futato

Printing History:

February 2004:   First Edition.

0-596-00628-4
[C]   [6/04]

Contents

What's in This Book?   1
    What's Linux?   2
    What's Fedora Linux?   2
    What's a Command?   3
    Users and Superusers   4
    Reading This Book   5

Getting Help   7

Fedora: A First View   9
    The Role of the Shell   10
    How to Run a Shell   11

Logins, Logouts, and Shutdowns   11

The Filesystem   13
    Home Directories   14
    System Directories   15
    Operating System Directories   18
    File Protections   19

The Shell   20
    The Shell Versus Programs   21
    Selected bash Features   21
    Job Control   29

Killing a Command in Progress	32
Terminating a Shell	33
Tailoring Shell Behavior	33
Installing Software	**33**
Basic File Operations	**37**
Directory Operations	**41**
File Viewing	**43**
File Creation and Editing	**51**
File Properties	**56**
File Location	**65**
File Text Manipulation	**71**
File Compression and Packaging	**82**
File Comparison	**86**
Disks and Filesystems	**91**
Backups and Remote Storage	**95**
File Printing	**101**
Spelling Operations	**102**
Viewing Processes	**104**
Controlling Processes	**108**
Users and Their Environment	**110**
Working with User Accounts	**115**

Becoming the Superuser   118

Working with Groups   119

Basic Host Information   121

Host Location   124

Network Connections   128

Email   132

Web Browsing   136

Usenet News   140

Instant Messaging   142

Screen Output   144

Math and Calculations   149

Dates and Times   152

Scheduling Jobs   155

Graphics and Screensavers   160

Audio and Video   163

Programming with Shell Scripts   166
    Whitespace and Linebreaks   166
    Variables   166
    Input and Output   167
    Booleans and Return Codes   167
    Conditionals   170
    Loops   172
    Break and Continue   174

Creating and Running Shell Scripts   176
Command-Line Arguments   177
Exiting with a Return Code   178
Beyond Shell Scripting   178

Final Words   **179**
Acknowledgments   179

Linux Pocket Guide

Welcome to Linux! If you're a new user, this book can serve as a quick introduction to Linux in general, and Fedora Linux specifically, as well as a guide to common and practical commands. If you have Linux experience, feel free to skip the introductory material.

What's in This Book?

This book is a short guide, *not a comprehensive reference*. We cover important, useful aspects of Linux so you can work productively. We do not, however, present every single command and every last option (our apologies if your favorite was omitted), nor delve into detail about operating system internals. Short, sweet, and essential, that's our motto.

We focus on *commands*, those pesky little words you type on a command line to tell a Linux system what to do, like ls (list files), grep (search for text in a file), xmms (play audio files), and df (measure free disk space). We touch briefly on graphical windowing environments like GNOME and KDE, each of which could fill a Pocket Guide by itself.

We've organized the material by function to provide a concise learning path. For example, to help you view the contents of a file, we introduce all file-viewing commands together: cat for short text files, less for longer ones, od for binary files, ghostview for Postscript, and so on. Then we explain each of these commands in turn, briefly presenting its common uses and options.

We assume you have an account on a Linux system and know how to log in with your username and password. If not, speak with your system administrator, or if the system is your own, use the account created when you installed Linux.

What's Linux?

Linux is a popular, open-source computer software environment that competes with Microsoft Windows and the Apple Macintosh. It has four major parts:

The kernel
> The low-level operating system, handling files, disks, networking, and other necessities we take for granted.

Supplied programs
> Thousands of programs for file manipulation, text editing, mathematics, typesetting, audio, video, computer programming, web site creation, encryption, CD burning... you name it.

The shell
> A user interface for typing commands, executing them, and displaying the results. There are various shells in existence: the Bourne shell, Korn shell, C shell, and others. This book focuses on bash, the Bourne Again Shell, which is often the default for user accounts. However, all these shells have similar basic functions.

X
> A graphical system that provides windows, menus, icons, mouse support, and other familiar GUI elements. More complex graphical environments are built on X; the most popular are KDE and GNOME. Throughout this book, we discuss programs that open their own X windows to run.

What's Fedora Linux?

Fedora Linux is one particular Linux *distribution* or "distro," created by Red Hat, Inc. and the Fedora project (for more information, see *http://fedora.redhat.com*) and formerly called Red Hat Linux.* Our material is based on Fedora Core 1, the first official release (November 2003). We focus on the supplied programs and the shell, with brief coverage of X and the kernel as needed.

What's a Command?

A Linux command typically consists of a *program name* followed by *options* and *arguments*, typed within a shell. The program name refers to a program somewhere on disk (which the shell will locate and run). Options, which usually begin with a dash, affect the behavior of the program, and arguments usually represent inputs and outputs. For example, this command to count the lines in a file:

```
$ wc -l myfile
```

consists of a program (wc, the "word count" program), an option (-l) saying to count lines, and an argument (*myfile*) indicating the file to read. (The dollar sign is a *prompt* from the shell, indicating that it is waiting for your command.) Options may be given individually:

```
$ myprogram -a -b -c myfile          Three individual options
```

or combined behind a single dash:

```
$ myprogram -abc myfile              Same as -a -b -c
```

though some programs are quirky and do not recognize combined options.

Commands can also be much more complex than running a single program:

- They can run several programs at once, either in sequence (one after the other) or connected into a "pipeline" with the output of one command becoming the input of the next.

---

* Red Hat now focuses on its Enterprise Linux products for higher-end applications. Most of this book applies to Enterprise and other Linux distros.

- Options are not standardized. The same option (say, -l) may have different meanings to different programs: in wc -l it means "count lines of text," but in ls -l it means "produce longer output." In the other direction, two programs might use different options to mean the same thing, such as -q for "run quietly" versus -s for "run silently."

- Likewise, arguments are not standardized. They often represent filenames for input or output, but they can be other things too, like directory names or regular expressions.

- The Linux command-line user interface—the *shell*—has a programming language built in. So instead of a command saying "run this program," it might say, "if today is Tuesday, run this program, otherwise run another command six times for each file whose name ends in *.txt.*"

Users and Superusers

Linux is a multiuser operating system. On a given computer, each user is identified by a unique *username*, like "smith" or "funkyguy," and owns a (reasonably) private part of the system for doing work. There is also a specially designated user, with username *root*, who has the privileges to do anything at all on the system. Ordinary users are restricted: though they can run most programs, in general they can modify only the files they own. The superuser, on the other hand, can create, modify, or delete any file and run any program.

Some commands in this book can be run successfully only by the superuser. In this case, we use a hash mark (#) as the shell prompt:

```
# command goes here
```

Otherwise, we will use the dollar sign prompt indicating an ordinary user:

```
$ command goes here
```

To become the superuser, you needn't log out and log back in; just run the su command (see "Becoming the Superuser" on page 118) and provide the superuser password:

```
$ su -l
Password: ********
#
```

Reading This Book

When we describe a command, we first present its general usage information. For example, the wc (word count) program has the general usage:

```
wc [options] [files]
```

which means you'd type "wc" followed, if you choose, by options and then filenames. You wouldn't type the square brackets "[" and "]": they just indicate their contents are optional; and words in italics mean you have to fill in your own specific values, like names of actual files. If you see a vertical bar between options or arguments, perhaps grouped by parentheses:

```
ls (file | directory)
```

this indicates choice: when running the ls command, you may supply either a file or directory name as an argument.

Input and output

Most Linux programs accept data from *standard input*, which is usually your keyboard, and produce output on *standard output*, which is usually your screen. Additionally, error messages are usually displayed on *standard error*, which also is usually your screen but kept separate from standard output.* Later we'll see how to *redirect* standard input, output, and error to and from files or pipes. But let's get our vocabulary straight. When we say a command "reads," we mean from

---

* For example, you can capture standard output in a file and still have standard error messages appear on screen.

standard input unless we say otherwise. And when a command "prints," we mean on standard output, unless we're talking about computer printers.

Standard heading

Each command description begins with a heading like this one for the ls (list files) command.

ls [*options*] [*files*] coreutils

/bin	stdin	stdout	- file	-- opt	--help	--version

The heading includes the command name (ls) and usage, the directory in which it is located (*/bin*), the RPM package that installed the command (*coreutils*), and six properties of the command printed in black (supported) or gray (unsupported):

stdin
> The command reads from standard input, i.e., your keyboard, by default.

stdout
> The command writes to standard output, i.e., your screen, by default.

- file
> If you supply a dash (-) argument in place of an input filename, the command reads from standard input; and likewise, if the dash is supplied as an output filename, the command writes to standard output. For example, the following wc (word count) command line reads the files *file1* and *file2*, then standard input, then *file3*:
>
> ```
> $ wc file1 file2 - file3
> ```

-- opt
> If you supply the command-line option "--" it means "end of options": anything appearing later on the command line is not an option. This is sometimes necessary to operate on a file whose name begins with a dash, which otherwise would be (mistakenly) treated as an option. For example, if you have a file named *-foo*, the command wc -foo will fail because *-foo* will be treated as an (invalid) option. wc -- -foo works. If a command does not support "--", you can prepend the current

directory path "./" to the filename so the dash is no longer the first character:

```
$ wc ./-foo
```

--help
> The option --help makes the command print a help message explaining proper usage, then exit.

--version
> The option --version makes the command print its version number and exit.

Standard symbols

Throughout the book, we use certain symbols to indicate keystrokes. Like many other Linux documents, we use the ^ symbol to mean "press and hold the control (Ctrl) key," so for example, ^D (pronounced "control D") means "press and hold the control key and type D." We also write ESC to mean "press the Escape key." Keys like Enter and Spacebar should be self-explanatory.

Your friend, the echo command

In many of our examples, we'll print information to the screen with the echo command, which we'll formally describe in "Screen Output" on page 144. echo is one of the simplest commands: it merely prints its arguments on standard output, once those arguments have been processed by the shell.

```
$ echo My dog has fleas
My dog has fleas
$ echo My name shell is $USER        Shell variable USER
My name is smith
```

Getting Help

If you need more information than this book provides, there are several things you can do.

Run the man command

The man command displays an online manual page, or *manpage*, for a given program. For example, to get documentation on listing files with ls, run:

```
$ man ls
```

To search for manpages by keyword for a particular topic, use the -k option followed by the keyword:

```
$ man -k database
```

Run the info command

The info command is an extended, hypertext help system covering many Linux programs.

```
$ info ls
```

If no documentation is found on a given program, info displays the program's manpage. For a listing of available documentation, type info by itself. To learn how to navigate the info system, type info info.

Use the --help option (if any)

Many Linux commands respond to the option --help by printing a short help message. Try:

```
$ ls --help
```

Examine the directory /usr/share/doc

This directory contains supporting documents for many programs, usually organized by program name and version. For example, files for the text editor Emacs, Version 21.3, are found in */usr/share/doc/emacs-21.3*.

GNOME and KDE Help

For help with GNOME or KDE, choose the Help item in the main menu.

Fedora-specific web sites

The official site is *http://fedora.redhat.com*. An unofficial FAQ has sprung up at *http://fedora.artoo.net*. And of course there's the web site for this book:

http://www.oreilly.com/catalog/linuxpg/

Usenet newsgroups

Usenet has dozens of newsgroups on Linux topics, such as *comp.os.linux.misc* and *comp.os.linux.questions*. For Red Hat-specific information, try *alt.os.linux.redhat*, *comp.os.linux.redhat*, *linux.redhat*, and *linux.redhat.misc*. You can search through newsgroup postings at Google Groups, *http://groups.google.com*, which is a goldmine of troubleshooting information.

Google

Search Google for further documentation and tutorials at *http://www.google.com* (if you've been living in a closet).

Fedora: A First View

When you log into a Fedora (or other) Linux system, you're likely to be greeted by a graphical desktop[*] like Figure 1, which contains:

- A Windows-like taskbar across the bottom, with:
  - A "red hat" icon in the lower left, which when clicked, pops up a main menu of programs
  - Icons to run various programs, such as the Mozilla web browser, Evolution email program, and Print Manager for configuring printers
  - A desktop switcher (the square with four boxes in it), which lets you maintain and switch between multiple desktops
  - A blue checkmark indicating that your system software is up to date, or a red exclamation point warning you that it isn't
  - A clock
- Other icons on the desktop, such as a trash can for deleting files, a floppy disk, and your home directory (folder) for storing personal files

---

[*] Unless you're logging in remotely over the network, in which case you'll see a command line, prompting you to type a command.

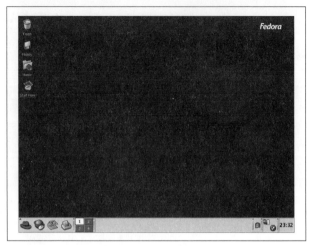

Figure 1. Fedora graphical desktop

Fedora comes with several similar-looking interfaces, and the one you're viewing is either GNOME or KDE.* You can tell the difference by clicking the red hat icon to bring up the main menu, and choosing Help. The Help window that appears will clearly indicate GNOME or KDE.

The Role of the Shell

Explore the environment of icons and menus in GNOME and KDE. These graphical interfaces are, for some users, the primary way to compute with Linux. Various distros, including Fedora, simplify these interfaces so users can edit files, read email, and browse the Web without much effort.

Nevertheless, the true power of Linux lies behind the scenes. To get the most out of Linux, you should become proficient

---

* Depending on your system configuration, the interface might look different. GNOME and KDE are very configurable, and Fedora includes a third interface, twm, with yet another look and feel. (And Linux has other graphical interfaces, too.)

in using the shell. It might initially be more difficult than icons and menus, but once you're used to it, the shell is quite easy to use and very powerful. Most of this book discusses Linux commands run via the shell.

How to Run a Shell

To run a shell within GNOME, KDE, or any other graphical interface for Linux, you'll need to open a *shell window*. This is done by programs like xterm, gnome-terminal, konsole, and uxterm. Each of these programs does the same basic thing: open a window that is running a shell, awaiting your input. To run a shell window using the three default windowing interfaces for Fedora:

Interface	Take this action...	...to run this shell window program
GNOME	Menu : System Tools : Terminal *or on the desktop:* Right Mouse Button : Open Terminal	gnome-terminal
KDE	Menu : System Tools : Terminal *or on the desktop:* Right Mouse Button : Open Terminal	konsole
twm	*On the desktop:* Right Mouse Button : XTerm	xterm

Don't confuse the window program (like konsole) with the shell running inside it. The window is just a container—albeit with fancy features of its own—but the shell is what prompts you for commands and runs them.

If you're not running a graphical interface—say, you're logging in remotely over the network, or directly over an attached terminal—a shell will run immediately when you log in. No shell window is required.

Logins, Logouts, and Shutdowns

We assume you know how to log into your Linux account. To log out from GNOME or KDE, click the red hat icon in the

---

taskbar and choose Logout from the main menu. To log out from a remote shell, just close the shell (type exit or logout).

Never simply turn off the power to a Linux system: it needs a more graceful shutdown. To perform a shutdown from GNOME, choose Logout → Shut Down. From KDE, first log out, then on the login screen, click the Shutdown icon. To perform a shutdown from a shell, run the shutdown command as the superuser, as follows.

shutdown [*options*] *time* [*message*]   SysVinit

/sbin		stdin	**stdout**	- file	-- opt	--help	--version

The shutdown command halts or reboots a Linux system; only the superuser may run it. Here's a command to halt the system in 10 minutes, broadcasting the message "scheduled maintenance" to all users logged in:

```
# shutdown -h +10 "scheduled maintenance"
```

The *time* may be a number of minutes preceded by a plus sign, like +10, an absolute time in hours and minutes, like 16:25, or the word now to mean immediately.

With no options, shutdown puts the system into single-user mode, a special maintenance mode in which only one person is logged in (at the system console), and all nonessential services are off. To exit single-user mode, either perform another shutdown to halt or reboot, or type ^D to bring up the system in normal, multiuser mode.

Useful options

-r	Reboot the system.
-h	Halt the system.
-k	Kidding: don't really perform a shutdown, just broadcast warning messages to all users as if the system were going down.
-c	Cancel a shutdown in progress (omit the *time* argument).
-f	On reboot, skip the usual filesystem check performed by the fsck program (described in "Disks and Filesystems" on page 91).
-F	On reboot, require the usual filesystem check.

For technical information about shutdowns, single-user mode, and various system states, see the manpages for `init` and `inittab`.

The Filesystem

To make use of any Linux system, you need to be comfortable with Linux files and their layout. Every Linux file is contained in a collection called a *directory*. Directories are like folders on Windows and Macintosh systems. Directories form a hierarchy, or *tree*: one directory may contain other directories, called *subdirectories*, which may themselves contain other files and subdirectories, and so on, into infinity. The topmost directory is called the *root directory* and is denoted by a slash (/).[*]

We refer to files and directories using a "names and slashes" syntax called a *path*. For instance, this path:

    /one/two/three/four

refers to the root directory /, which contains a directory called *one*, which contains a directory *two*, which contains a directory *three*, which contains a final file or directory, *four*. If a path begins with the root directory, it's called an *absolute* path, and if not, it's a *relative* path. More on this in a moment.

Whenever you are running a shell, that shell is "in" some directory (in an abstract sense). More technically, your shell has a *current working directory*, and when you run commands in that shell, they operate relative (there's that word again) to the directory. More specifically, if you refer to a relative file path in that shell, it is relative to your current working directory. For example, if your shell is "in" the directory */one/two/three*, and you run a command that refers to a file *myfile*, then it's really

---

[*] In Linux, *all* files and directories descend from the root. This is unlike Windows or DOS, in which different devices are accessed by drive letters.

/one/two/three/myfile. Likewise, a relative path *a/b/c* would imply the true path */one/two/three/a/b/c*.

Two special directories are denoted . (a single period) and .. (two periods in a row). The former means your current directory, and the latter means your *parent* directory, one level above. So if your current directory is */one/two/three*, then . refers to this directory and .. refers to */one/two*.

You "move" your shell from one directory to another using the cd command:

```
$ cd /one/two/three
```

More technically, this command changes your shell's current working directory to be */one/two/three*. This is an absolute change (since the directory begins with "/"); of course you can make relative moves as well:

```
$ cd d              Enter subdirectory d
$ cd ../mydir       Go up to my parent, then into directory mydir
```

File and directory names may contain most characters you expect: capital and small letters,* numbers, periods, dashes, underscores, and most other symbols (just not "/"; it's reserved for separating directories). In general, however, avoid using spaces, asterisks, parentheses, and other characters that have special meaning to the shell. Otherwise, you'll need to quote or escape these characters all the time. (See "Quoting" on page 27.)

Home Directories

Users' personal files are often found in */home* (for ordinary users) or */root* (for superusers). Your home directory is typically */home/your-username: /home/smith, /home/jones*, etc. There are several ways to locate or refer to your home directory.

cd
> With no arguments, the cd command returns you (i.e., sets the shell's working directory) to your home directory.

---

* These are not equivalent, since Linux filenames are case-sensitive.

HOME variable

The environment variable HOME (see "Shell variables" on page 23) contains the name of your home directory.

```
$ echo $HOME        The echo command prints its arguments
/home/smith
```

~

When used in place of a directory, a lone tilde is expanded by the shell to the name of your home directory.

```
$ echo ~
/home/smith
```

When followed by a username (as in *~smith*), the shell expands this string to be the user's home directory:

```
$ cd ~smith
$ pwd               The "print working directory" command
/home/smith
```

System Directories

A typical Linux system has tens of thousands of system directories. These directories contain operating system files, applications, documentation, and just about everything *except* private user files (which typically live in */home*).

Unless you're a system administrator, you'll rarely visit most system directories—but with a little knowledge you can understand or guess their purposes. Their names often contain three parts, which we'll call the scope, category, and application. (These are not standard terms, but they'll help you understand things.) For example, the directory */usr/local/share/emacs*, which contains local data for the Emacs text editor, has scope */usr/local* (locally installed system files), category *share* (program-specific data and documentation), and application *emacs* (a text editor), shown in Figure 2. We'll explain these three parts, slightly out of order.

Figure 2. Directory scope, category, and application

Directory path part 1: category

A *category* tells you the types of files found in a directory. For example, if the category is *bin*, you can be reasonably assured that the directory contains programs. Common categories are listed below.

Categories for programs

bin	Programs (usually binary files)
sbin	Programs (usually binary files) intended to be run by the superuser, root
lib	Libraries of code used by programs
libexec	Programs invoked by other programs, not usually by users; think "library of executable programs"

Categories for documentation

doc	Documentation
info	Documentation files for Emacs's built-in help system
man	Documentation files (manual pages) displayed by the man program; the files are often compressed, or sprinkled with typesetting commands for man to interpret
share	Program-specific files, such as examples and installation instructions

Categories for configuration

etc	Configuration files for the system (and other miscellaneous stuff)
init.d *rc.d*	Configuration files for booting Linux; also *rc1.d*, *rc2.d*, ...

Categories for programming

include	Header files for programming
src	Source code for programs

Categories for web files

cgi-bin	Scripts/programs that run on web pages
html	Web pages
public_html	Web pages, typically in users' home directories
www	Web pages

Categories for display

fonts	Fonts (surprise!)
X11	X window system files

Categories for hardware

dev	Device files for interfacing with disks and other hardware
mnt *misc*	Mount points: directories that provide access to disks

Categories for runtime files

var	Files specific to this computer, created and updated as the computer runs
lock	Lock files, created by programs to say, "I am running;" the existence of a lock file may prevent another program, or another instance of the same program, from running or performing an action
log	Log files that track important system events, containing error, warning, and informational messages
mail	Mailboxes for incoming mail
run	PID files, which contain the IDs of running processes; these files are often consulted to track or kill particular processes
spool	Files queued or in transit, such as outgoing email, print jobs, and scheduled jobs
tmp	Temporary storage for programs and/or people to use
proc	Operating system state: see "Operating System Directories" on page 18

Directory path part 2: scope

The *scope* of a directory path describes, at a high level, the purpose of an entire directory hierarchy. Some common ones are:

/	System files supplied with Linux (pronounced "root")
/usr	More system files supplied with Linux (pronounced "user")
/usr/games	Games (surprise!)
/usr/kerberos	Files pertaining to the Kerberos authentication system
/usr/local	System files developed "locally," either for your organization or your individual computer
/usr/X11R6	Files pertaining to the X window system

So for a category like *lib* (libraries), your Linux system might have directories */lib*, */usr/lib*, */usr/local/lib*, */usr/games/lib*, and */usr/X11R6/lib*. You might have other scopes as suits the system administrator: */my-company/lib*, */my-division/lib*, and so on.

There isn't a clear distinction between / and /usr in practice, but there is a sense that / is "lower-level" and closer to the operating system. So /bin contains fundamental programs like ls and cat, /usr/bin contains a wide variety of applications supplied with your Linux distribution, and /usr/local/bin contains programs your system administrator chose to install. These are not hard-and-fast rules but typical cases.

Directory path part 3: application

The application part of a directory path is usually the name of a program. After the scope and category (say, /usr/local/doc), a program may have its own subdirectory (say, /usr/local/doc/myprogram) containing files it needs.

Operating System Directories

/boot
> Files for booting the system. This is where the kernel lives, typically named /boot/vmlinuz.

/lost+found
> Damaged files that were rescued by a disk recovery tool.

/proc
> Describes currently-running processes; for advanced users.

The files in /proc provide views into the running kernel and have special properties. They always appear to be zero sized, read-only, and dated now:

```
$ ls -l /proc/version
-r--r--r--  1 root    root     0 Oct  3 22:55 /proc/version
```

However, their contents magically contain information about the Linux kernel:

```
$ cat /proc/version
Linux version 2.4.22-1.2115.nptl ...
```

Mostly these files are used by programs. Go ahead and explore. Here are some examples.

/proc/ioports	A list of your computer's input/output hardware.
/proc/version	The operating system version. The uname command prints the same information.
/proc/uptime	System uptime, i.e., seconds elapsed since the system was last booted. Run the uptime command for a more human-readable result.
/proc/nnn	Where *nnn* is a positive integer, information about the Linux process with process ID *nnn*.
/proc/self	Information about the current process you're running; a symbolic link to a */proc/nnn* file, automatically updated. Try ls -l /proc/self a few times in a row: you'll see */proc/self* changing where it points.

File Protections

A Linux system may have many users with login accounts. To maintain privacy and security, each user can access only *some* files on the system, not all. This access control is embodied in two questions:

Who has permission?   Every file and directory has an *owner* who has permission to do anything with it. Typically the user who created a file is its owner, but relationships can get more complex.

Additionally, a predefined *group* of users may have permission to access a file. Groups are defined by the system administrator and are covered in "Working with Groups" on page 119.

Finally, a file or directory can be opened to *all users* with login accounts on the system. You'll also see this set of users called *the world* or simply *other*.

What kind of permission is granted?   File owners, groups, and the world may each have permission to *read*, *write* (modify), and *execute* (run) particular files. Permissions also extend to directories, which users may read (access files within the directory), write (create and delete files within the directory), and execute (enter the directory).

To see the ownership and permissions of a file, run:

```
$ ls -l filename
```

To see the ownership and permissions of a directory, run:

```
$ ls -ld directory_name
```

The file permissions are the 10 leftmost characters in the output, a string of r (read), w (write), x (execute), and other letters. For example:

```
drwxr-x---
```

Here's what these letters and symbols mean.

Position	Meaning
1	File type: - = file, d = directory, l = symbolic link, p = named pipe, c = character device, b = block device
2–4	Read, write, and execute permissions for the file's owner
5–7	Read, write, and execute permissions for the file's group
8–10	Read, write, and execute permissions for all other users

We describe ls in more detail in "Basic File Operations" on page 37. To change the owner, group ownership, or permissions of a file, use the chown, chgrp, and chmod commands, respectively, as described in "File Properties" on page 56.

The Shell

In order to run commands on a Linux system, you'll need somewhere to type them. That "somewhere" is called the *shell*, which is Linux's command-line user interface: you type a command and press Enter, and the shell runs whatever program (or programs) you've requested. To run a shell, see "Fedora: A First View" on page 9.

For example, to see who's logged in, you could execute this command in a shell:

```
$ who
barrett      :0     Sep 23 20:44
byrnes    pts/0     Sep 15 13:51
silver    pts/1     Sep 22 21:15
silver    pts/2     Sep 22 21:18
```

(The dollar sign is the shell prompt, which means the shell is ready to run a command.) A single command can also invoke several programs at the same time, and even connect programs together so they interact. Here's a command that redirects the output of the who program to become the input of the wc program, which counts lines of text in a file; the result is the number of lines in the output of who:

```
$ who | wc -l
4
```

telling you how many users are logged in.* The vertical bar, called a *pipe*, makes the connection between who and wc.

A shell is actually a program itself, and Linux has several. We focus on Bash (the "Bourne-Again Shell"), located in */bin/bash*, which is the Fedora Linux default.

The Shell Versus Programs

When you run a command, it might invoke a Linux program (like who), or instead it might be a *built-in command*, a feature of the shell itself. You can tell the difference with the type command:

```
$ type who
who is /usr/bin/who
$ type cd
cd is a shell builtin
```

It is helpful to know what the shell provides versus what Linux does. The next few sections describe features of the shell.

Selected bash Features

A shell does much more than simply run commands. It also provides powerful features to make this task easier. Examples

---

* Actually, how many interactive shells those users are running. If a user has several shells running, like the user silver in our example, they'll have that many lines of output in who.

---

are wildcards for matching filenames, redirection of command output and input to and from files, pipes for making the output of one command become the input of another, aliases to run common commands quickly, variables for storing values for use by the shell, and more. We're just scratching the surface to introduce you to a set of useful tools. Run info bash for full documentation.

Wildcards

Wildcards provide a shorthand for specifying sets of files with similar names. For example, a* means all files whose names begin with lowercase "a". Wildcards are "expanded" by the shell into the actual set of filenames they match. So if you type:

```
$ ls a*
```

the shell first expands a* into the filenames that begin with "a" in your current directory, as if you had typed:

```
ls aardvark adamantium apple
```

ls never knows you used a wildcard: it sees only the final list of filenames after the shell expansion.

Wildcard	Meaning
*	Any set of characters except a leading period
?	Any single character
[set]	Any single character in the given set, most commonly a sequence of characters, like [aeiouAEIOU] for all vowels, or a range with a dash, like [A-Z] for all capital letters
[^set] [!set]	Any single character not in the given set (as above)

When using sets, if you want to include a literal dash in the set, put it first or last. To include a literal closing square bracket in the set, put it first. To include a ^ or ! literally, don't put it first.

Brace expansion

Similar to wildcards, expressions with curly braces also expand to become multiple arguments to a command. The comma-separated expression:

```
{a,b,cc,ddd}
```

expands to:

```
a b cc dddd
```

Braces work with any strings, unlike wildcards which are limited to filenames. For example, sand{X,Y,ZZZ}wich expands to:

```
$ echo sand{X,Y,ZZZ}wich
sandXwich sandYwich sandZZZwich
```

regardless of what files are in the current directory.

Tilde expansion

The shell treats tildes (~) as special characters if they appear alone or at the beginning of a word.

~	Your home directory
~smith	User smith's home directory

Shell variables

You can define variables and their values by assigning them:

```
$ MYVAR=3
```

To refer to a value, simply place a dollar sign in front of the variable name:

```
$ echo $MYVAR
3
```

Some variables are standard and commonly defined by your shell upon login.

Variable	Meaning
DISPLAY	The name of your X window display
HOME	The name of your home directory

Variable	Meaning
LOGNAME	Your login name
MAIL	Path your incoming mailbox
OLDPWD	Your shell's previous directory
PATH	Your shell search path: directories separated by colons
PWD	Your shell's current directory
SHELL	The path to your shell, e.g., */bin/bash*
TERM	The type of your terminal, e.g., xterm or vt100
USER	Your login name

To see a shell's variables, run:

```
$ printenv
```

The scope of the variable (i.e., which programs know about it) is, by default, the shell in which it's defined. To make a variable and its value available to other programs your shell invokes (i.e., subshells), use the export command:

```
$ export MYVAR
```

or the shorthand:

```
$ export MYVAR=3
```

Your variable is now called an *environment variable*, since it's available to other programs in your shell's "environment." To make a specific value available to a specific program just once, prepend *variable=value* to the command line:

```
$ echo $HOME
/home/smith
$ HOME=/home/sally echo "My home is $HOME"
My home is /home/sally
$ echo $HOME
/home/smith                    The original value is unaffected
```

Search path

A very important variable is PATH, which instructs the shell where to find programs. When you type any command:

```
$ who
```

the shell has to find the program(s) in question. It consults the value of PATH, which is a sequence of directories separated by colons:

```
$ echo $PATH
/usr/local/bin:/bin:/usr/bin:/usr/X11R6/bin:/home/smith/bin
```

and looks for the who command in each of these directories. If it finds who (say, */usr/bin/who*), it runs the command. Otherwise, it reports:

```
bash: who: command not found
```

To add directories to your shell's search path temporarily, modify its PATH variable. For example, to append */usr/sbin* to your shell's search path:

```
$ PATH=$PATH:/usr/sbin
$ echo $PATH
/usr/local/bin:/bin:/usr/bin:/usr/X11R6/bin:/home/smith/
bin:/usr/sbin
```

To make this change permanent, modify the PATH variable in your startup file ~/.*bash_profile*, as explained in "Tailoring Shell Behavior" on page 33. Then log out and log back in.

Aliases

The built-in command alias defines a convenient shorthand for a longer command, to save typing. For example:

```
$ alias ll='ls -l'
```

defines a new command ll that runs ls -l:

```
$ ll
total 436
-rw-r--r--    1 smith     3584 Oct 11 14:59 file1
-rwxr-xr-x    1 smith       72 Aug  6 23:04 file2
...
```

Define aliases in your ~/.*bashrc* file (see "Tailoring Shell Behavior" on page 33) to be available whenever you log in. To see all your aliases, type alias. If aliases don't seem powerful enough for you (since they have no parameters or branching), see

"Programming with Shell Scripts" on page 166, run info bash, and read up on "shell functions."

Input/output redirection

The shell can redirect standard input, standard output, and standard error to and from files. In other words, any command that reads from standard input can have its input come from a file instead with the shell's < operator:

```
$ mycommand < infile
```

Likewise, any command that writes to standard output can write to a file instead:

```
$ mycommand > outfile        Create/overwrite outfile
$ mycommand >> outfile       Append to outfile
```

A command that writes to standard error can have its output redirected to a file as well:

```
$ mycommand 2> errorfile
```

To redirect both standard output and standard error to files:

```
$ mycommand > outfile 2> errorfile     Separate files
$ mycommand > outfile 2>&1             Single file
```

Pipes

Using the shell, you can redirect the standard output of one command to be the standard input of another, using the shell's pipe (|) operator. For example:

```
$ who | sort
```

sends the output of who into the sort program, printing an alphabetically sorted list of logged-in users.

Combining commands

To invoke several commands in sequence on a single command line, separate them with semicolons:

```
$ command1 ; command2 ; command3
```

To run a sequence of commands as above, but stop execution if any of them fails, separate them with && ("and") symbols:

```
$ command1 && command2 && command3
```

To run a sequence of commands, stopping execution as soon as one succeeds, separate them with || ("or") symbols:

```
$ command1 || command2 || command3
```

Quoting

Normally, the shell treats whitespace simply as separating the words on the command line. If you want a word to *contain* whitespace (e.g., a filename with a space in it), surround it with single or double quotes to make the shell treat it as a unit. Single quotes treat their contents literally, while double quotes let shell constructs be evaluated, such as variables:

```
$ echo 'The variable HOME has value $HOME'
The variable HOME has value $HOME
$ echo "The variable HOME has value $HOME"
The variable HOME has value /home/smith
```

Backquotes cause their contents to be evaluated as a command; the contents are then replaced by the standard output of the command:

```
$ /usr/bin/whoami
smith
$ echo My name is `/usr/bin/whoami`
My name is smith
```

Escaping

If a character has special meaning to the shell but you want it used literally (e.g., * as a literal asterisk rather than a wildcard), precede the character with the forward slash "\" character. This is called *escaping* the special character:

```
$ echo a*                    As a wildcard, matching "a" filenames
aardvark  agnostic  apple
$ echo a\*                   As a literal asterisk
a*
```

```
$ echo "I live in $HOME"        Dollar sign means a variable value
I live in /home/smith
$ echo "I live in \$HOME"       A literal dollar sign
I live in $HOME
```

You can also escape control characters (tabs, newlines, ^D, and so forth) to have them used literally on the command line, if you precede them with ^V. This is particularly useful for tab (^I) characters, which the shell would otherwise use for filename completion (see "Filename completion" on page 29).

```
$ echo "There is a tab between here^V^Iand here"
There is a tab between here        and here
```

Command-line editing

bash lets you edit the command line you're working on, using keystrokes inspired by the text editors emacs and vi (see "File Creation and Editing" on page 51). To enable command-line editing with emacs keys, run this command (and place it in your ~/.bash_profile to make it permanent):

```
$ set -o emacs
```

For vi keys:

```
$ set -o vi
```

emacs keystroke	vi keystroke (first type ESC)	Meaning
^P or up arrow	k	Previous command line
^N or down arrow	j	Next command line
^F or right arrow	l	Forward one character
^B or left arrow	h	Backward one character
^A	0	Beginning of line
^E	$	End of line
^D	x	Delete next character
^U	^U	Erase entire line

Command history

You can recall previous commands you've run—that is, the shell's *history*—and then edit and re-execute them. Some useful history-related commands are listed below.

Command	Meaning
`history`	Print your history
`history N`	Print the most recent *N* commands in your history
`history -c`	Clear (delete) your history
`!!`	Previous command
`!N`	Command number *N* in your history
`!-N`	The command you typed *N* commands ago

`!$`	The last parameter from the previous command; great for checking that files are present before removing them:
	`$ ls a*`
	`$ rm !$`

`!*`	All parameters from the previous command

Filename completion

Press the TAB key while you are in the middle of typing a filename, and the shell will automatically complete (finish typing) the filename for you. If several filenames match what you've typed so far, the shell will beep, indicating the match is ambiguous. Immediately press TAB again and the shell will present the alternatives. Try this:

```
$ cd /usr/bin
$ ls un<TAB><TAB>
```

Job Control

`jobs`	List your jobs
`&`	Run a job in the background
`^Z`	Suspend the current (foreground) job
`suspend`	Suspend a shell
`fg`	Unsuspend a job: bring it into the foreground
`bg`	Make a suspended job run in the background

All Linux shells have *job control*: the ability to run programs in the background (multitasking behind the scenes) and foreground (running as the active process at your shell prompt). A *job* is simply the shell's unit of work. When you run a command interactively, your current shell tracks it as a job. When the command completes, the associated job disappears. Jobs are at a higher level than Linux processes; the Linux operating system knows nothing about them. They are merely constructs of the shell. Some important vocabulary about job control is:

foreground job
> Running in a shell, occupying the shell prompt so you cannot run another command

background job
> Running in a shell, but not occupying the shell prompt, so you can run another command in the same shell

suspend
> To stop a foreground job temporarily

resume
> To cause a suspended job to start running again

jobs

The built-in command jobs lists the jobs running in your current shell.

```
$ jobs
[1]-  Running               emacs myfile &
[2]+  Stopped               su
```

The integer on the left is the job number, and the plus sign identifies the default job affected by the fg (foreground) and bg (background) commands.

&

Placed at the end of a command-line, the ampersand causes the given command to run as a background job.

```
$ emacs myfile &
[2] 28090
```

The shell's response includes the job number (2) and the process ID of the command (28090).

^Z

Typing ^Z in a shell, while a job is running in the foreground, will suspend that job. It simply stops running, but its state is remembered.

```
$ mybigprogram
^Z
[1]+  Stopped                 mybigprogram
$
```

Now you're ready to type bg to put the command into the background, or fg to resume it in the foreground.

suspend

The built-in command suspend will suspend the current shell if possible, as if you'd typed ^Z to the shell itself. For instance, if you've run the su command and want to return to your original shell:

```
$ whoami
smith
$ su -l
Password: *******
# whoami
root
# suspend
[1]+  Stopped                 su
$ whoami
smith
```

bg [%jobnumber]

The built-in command bg sends a suspended job to run in the background. With no arguments, bg operates on the most recently suspended job. To specify a particular job (shown by the jobs command), supply the job number preceded by a percent sign:

```
$ bg %2
```

Some types of interactive jobs cannot remain in the background—
for instance, if they are waiting for input. If you try, the shell will
suspend the job and display:

```
[2]+  Stopped              command line here
```

You can now resume the job (with fg) and continue.

---

fg [%*jobnumber*]

The built-in command fg brings a suspended or backgrounded
job into the foreground. With no arguments, it selects a job,
usually the most recently suspended or backgrounded one. To
specify a particular job (as shown by the jobs command), supply
the job number preceded by a percent sign:

```
$ fg %2
```

Killing a Command in Progress

If you've launched a command from the shell running in the
foreground, and want to kill it immediately, type ^C. The shell
recognizes ^C as meaning, "terminate the current foreground
command right now." So if you are displaying a very long file
(say, with the cat command) and want to stop, type ^C:

```
$ cat bigfile
This is a very long file with many lines. Blah blah blah
blah blah blah blahblahblah ^C
$
```

To kill a program running in the background, you can bring
it into the foreground with fg and then type ^C, or alternatively, use the kill command (see "Controlling Processes"
on page 108).

In general, ^C is not a friendly way to end a program. If the
program has its own way to exit, use that when possible. You
see, ^C kills the program immediately, not giving it any
chance to clean up after itself. Killing a foreground program
may leave your shell in an odd or unresponsive state, perhaps not displaying the keystrokes you type. If this happens:

---

1. Press ^J to get a shell prompt. This produces the same character as the Enter key (a newline) but will work even if Enter does not.

2. Type the word reset (even if the letters don't appear while you type) and press ^J again to run this command. This should reset your shell.

^C works only when typed into a shell. It will likely have no effect if typed in a window that is not a shell window. Additionally, some programs are written to "catch" the ^C and ignore it: an example is the text editor emacs.

Terminating a Shell

To terminate a shell, either run the exit command or type ^D.*

```
$ exit
```

Tailoring Shell Behavior

To configure all your shells to work in a particular way, edit the files *.bash_profile* and *.bashrc* in your home directory. These files execute each time you log in (*~/.bash_profile*) or open a shell (*~/.bashrc*). They can set variables and aliases, run programs, print your horoscope, or whatever you like.

These two files are examples of *shell scripts*: executable files that contain shell commands. We'll cover this feature in more detail in "Programming with Shell Scripts" on page 166.

Installing Software

You will probably want to add further software to your Linux system from time to time. The most common forms of packaged software for Fedora and many other Linux distros are:

---

* Control-D indicates "end of file" to any program reading from standard input. In this case, the program is the shell itself, which terminates.

.rpm files

>Red Hat Package Manager (RPM) files. These are installed and managed with the programs rpm (manually) and up2date (automatically).

*.tar.gz files, *.tar.Z files, and *.tar.bz2 files*

>Compressed tar files. They are packaged with tar and compressed with gzip (.gz), compress (.Z), or bzip2 (.bz2).

Most new software must be installed by the superuser, so you'll need to run the su command (or equivalent) before installation. For example:

```
$ su -l
Password: ********
# rpm -ivh mypackage.rpm
...etc...
```

To locate new software, check your Linux CD-ROMs or visit fine sites like these:

>*http://freshmeat.net/*
>*http://freshrpms.net/*
>*http://rpmfind.net/*
>*http://sourceforge.net/*

up2date [*options*] [*packages*]   up2date

/usr/bin		stdin	**stdout**	- file	-- opt	--help	--version

up2date is the easiest way to keep your Fedora system... well, up to date. As root, just run:

```
# up2date
```

and follow the prompts. This provides a graphical user interface. You can also run up2date in command-line mode:

```
# up2date -l
```

to list all updated RPM packages (if any) available for your system. To download the given packages, run:

```
# up2date -d packages
```

To install the given RPM packages you have already down-loaded with up2date -d, run:

```
# up2date -i packages
```

up2date downloads RPM packages from Red Hat or Fedora-related servers over the Internet, so you might need to register your system with them the first time you run up2date.

Some Linux users prefer other programs to up2date, such as yum (*http://linux.duke.edu/projects/yum/*) and apt (*http://ayo. freshrpms.net/*).

rpm [*options*] [*files*]   rpm

/bin		stdin	**stdout**	- file	-- opt	--help	--version

If you prefer to install RPM packages by hand, use rpm, the same package-management program that up2date runs behind the scenes. rpm not only installs the software, but also makes sure your system has all prerequisites. For example, if package *superstuff* requires package *otherstuff* that you haven't installed, rpm will not install *superstuff*. If your system passes the test, however, rpm completely installs the software.

RPM filenames typically have the form *name-version. architecture*.rpm. For example, *emacs-20.7-17.i386.rpm* indicates the emacs package, Version 20.7-17, for i386 (Intel 80386 and higher) machines. Be aware that rpm sometimes requires a filename argument (like *emacs-20.7-17.i386.rpm*) and other times just the package name (like *emacs*).

Common commands for manipulating RPM packages are:

rpm -q *package_name*
    Find out if *package_name* is installed on your system, and what version. Example: rpm -q textutils. If you don't know the name of the package (a chicken-and-egg problem), list all packages and use grep to search for likely names:

```
$ rpm -qa | grep -i likely_name
```

`rpm -ql` *package_name*
> List the files included in the given, installed package. Try `rpm -ql emacs`.

`rpm -qi` *package_name*
> Get general information about the package.

`rpm -qlp` *package.rpm*
> List the contents of an RPM file, not necessarily installed yet. Use `-qip` for general information about the RPM file.

`rpm -qa`
> List all installed RPM packages. Useful for piping through grep to locate a package name:
>
> ```
> rpm -qa | grep -i emacs
> ```

`rpm -qf` *filename*
> Print the package that installed a given file on your system.
>
> ```
> $ rpm -qf /usr/bin/who
> sh-utils-2.0-11
> ```

`rpm -ivh` *package1*.rpm *package2*.rpm ...
> Install packages not already present on your system

`rpm -Fvh` *package1*.rpm *package2*.rpm ...
> Update packages that are already present on your system

`rpm -e` *package_names*
> Erase (delete) packages from your system. In this case, do not include the package version number, just the package name. For example, if you install the GNU Emacs package *emacs-20.7-17.i386.rpm*, you would uninstall it with `rpm -e emacs`, not `rpm -e emacs-20.7-17.rpm`.

tar.gz and tar.bz2 files

Packaged software files with names ending *.tar.gz* and *.tar.bz2* typically contain source code that you'll need to compile (build) before installation.

1. List the package contents, one file per line. Assure yourself that each file, when extracted, won't overwrite

something precious on your system, either accidentally
or maliciously:

```
$ tar tvzf package.tar.gz | less        For gzip files
$ tar tvjf package.tar.bz2 | less       For bzip2 files
```

2. If satisfied, extract the files into a new directory:

```
$ mkdir newdir
$ cd newdir
$ tar xvzf package.tar.gz               For gzip files
$ tar xvjf package.tar.bz2              For bzip2 files
```

3. Look for an extracted file named *INSTALL* or *README*.
   Read it to learn how to build the software, for example:

```
$ cd newdir
$ less INSTALL
```

4. Usually the *INSTALL* or *README* file will tell you to
   run a script called configure in the current directory,
   then run make, then run make install. Examine the
   options you may pass to the configure script:

```
$ ./configure --help
```

Then install the software:

```
$ ./configure options
$ make
$ su -l
Password: *******
# make install
```

Basic File Operations

ls	List files in a directory
cp	Copy a file
mv	Rename ("move") a file
rm	Delete ("remove") a file
ln	Create links (alternative names) to a file

One of the first things you'll need to do on a Linux system is
manipulate files: copying, renaming, deleting, and so forth.

ls [*options*] [*files*]

/bin   stdin   **stdout**   - file   -- opt   --help   --version

The ls command (pronounced as it is spelled, *ell ess*) lists attributes of files and directories. You can list files in the current directory:

    $ ls

in given directories:

    $ ls dir1 dir2 dir3

or individually:

    $ ls file1 file2 file3

The most important options are -a and -l. By default, ls hides files whose names begin with a dot; the -a option displays all files. The -l option produces a long listing:

    -rw-r--r--   1 smith users   149 Oct 28 2002 my.data

that includes, from left to right: the file's permissions (-rw-r--r--), owner (smith), group (users), size (149 bytes), last modification date (Oct 28 2002) and name. See "File Protections" on page 19 for more information on permissions.

Useful options

-a   List all files, including those whose names begin with a dot.

-l   Long listing, including file attributes. Add the -h option ("human-readable") to print file sizes in kilobytes, megabytes and gigabytes, instead of bytes.

-F   Decorate certain filenames with meaningful symbols, indicating their types. Appends "/" to directories, "*" to executables, "@" to symbolic links, "|" to named pipes, and "=" to sockets. These are just visual indicators for you, not part of the filenames!

-i   Prepend the inode numbers of the files.

-s   Prepend the size of the file in blocks, useful for sorting files by their size:

    $ ls -s | sort -n

-R   If listing a directory, list its contents recursively.

-d   If listing a directory, do not list its contents, just the directory itself.

cp *[options] files (file|dir)*

/bin			stdin	stdout	- file	-- opt	--help	--version

The cp command normally copies a file:

```
$ cp file file2
```

or copies multiple files into a directory:

```
$ cp file1 file2 file3 file4 dir
```

Using the -a or -R option, you can also recursively copy directories.

Useful options

-p   Copy not only the file contents, but also the file's permissions, timestamps, and if you have sufficient permission to do so, its owner and group. (Normally the copies will be owned by you, timestamped now, with permissions set by applying your umask to the original permissions.)

-a   Copy a directory hierarchy recursively, preserving special files, permissions, symbolic links, and hard link relationships. This combines the options -R (recursive copy including special files), -p (permissions), and -d (links).

-i   Interactive mode. Ask before overwriting destination files.

-f   Force the copy. If a destination file exists, overwrite it unconditionally.

mv *[options] source target*

/bin			stdin	stdout	- file	-- opt	--help	--version

The mv (move) command can rename a file:

```
$ mv file1 file2
```

or move files and directories into a destination directory:

```
$ mv file1 file2 dir3 dir4 destination_directory
```

Useful options

-i   Interactive mode. Ask before overwriting destination files.

-f   Force the move. If a destination file exists, overwrite it unconditionally.

rm *[options] files| directories*

/bin			stdin	stdout	- file	-- opt	--help	--version

The rm (remove) command can delete files:

```
$ rm file1 file2 file3
```

or recursively delete directories:

```
$ rm -r dir1 dir2
```

Useful options

-i	Interactive mode. Ask before deleting each file.
-f	Force the deletion, ignoring any errors or warnings.
-r	Recursively remove a directory and its contents. Use with caution, especially if combined with the -f option.

ln [*options*] *source target* coreutils

/bin	stdin	stdout	- file	-- opt	--help	--version

A *link* is a reference to another file, created by the ln command. There are two kinds of links. A *symbolic link* refers to another file by its path, much like a Windows "shortcut" or a Macintosh "alias."

```
$ ln -s myfile softlink
```

If you delete the original file, the now-dangling link will be invalid, pointing to a nonexistent file path. A *hard link*, on the other hand, is simply a second name for a physical file on disk (in tech talk, it points to the same inode). Deleting the original file does not invalidate the link.

```
$ ln myfile hardlink
```

Symbolic links can cross disk partitions, since they are just references to file paths; hard links cannot, since an inode on one disk has no meaning on another. Symbolic links can also point to directories, whereas hard links cannot... unless you are the superuser and use the -d option.

Useful options

-s	Make a symbolic link. The default is a hard link.
-i	Interactive mode. Ask before overwriting destination files.
-f	Force the link. If a destination file exists, overwrite it unconditionally.
-d	Allow the superuser to create a hard link to a directory.

It's easy find out where a symbolic link points with either of these commands:

```
$ readlink linkname
$ ls -l linkname
```

Directory Operations

cd	Change your current directory
pwd	Print the name of your current directory, i.e., "where you are now" in the filesystem
basename	Print the final part of a file path
dirname	Remove the final part of a file path
mkdir	Create a directory
rmdir	Delete an empty directory
rm -r	Delete a nonempty directory and its contents

We discussed the directory structure of Linux in "The Filesystem" on page 13. Now we'll cover commands that create, modify, delete, and manipulate directories within that structure.

cd [*directory*]   bash

shell built-in   stdin   stdout   - file   -- opt   --help   --version

The cd (change directory) command sets your current working directory. With no directory supplied, cd defaults to your home directory.

pwd   bash

shell built-in   stdin   **stdout**   - file   -- opt   --help   --version

The pwd command prints the absolute path of your current working directory:

```
$ pwd
/users/smith/mydir
```

basename *path*

/bin		stdin	**stdout**	- file	-- opt	--help	--version

The basename command prints the final component in a file path; so for the example above:

```
$ basename /users/smith/mydir
mydir
```

dirname *path*

coreutils

/usr/bin		stdin	**stdout**	- file	-- opt	--help	--version

The dirname command removes the final component from a file path:

```
$ dirname /users/smith/mydir
/users/smith
```

dirname simply manipulates a string that is a directory name. It does not change your current working directory.

mkdir [*options*] *directories*

coreutils

/bin		stdin	stdout	- file	-- opt	--help	--version

mkdir creates one or more directories:

```
$ mkdir d1 d2 d3
```

Useful options

-p If you supply a directory path (not just a simple directory name), create any necessary parent directories automatically: mkdir -p /one/two/three will create /one and /one/two if they don't already exist, then /one/two/three.

-m *mode* Create the directory with the given permissions:
```
$ mkdir 0755 mydir
```
By default, your shell's umask controls the permissions. See the chmod command in "File Properties" on page 56, and "File Protections" on page 19.

rmdir [*options*] *directories*

coreutils

/bin		stdin	stdout	- file	-- opt	--help	--version

The rmdir (remove directory) command deletes one or more empty directories you name. To delete a nonempty directory and its contents, use (carefully) rm -r *directory*. Use rm -ri *directory* to delete interactively, or `rm -rf` *directory* to annihilate without any error messages or confirmation.

Useful options

-p   If you supply a directory path (not just a simple directory name), delete not only the given directory, but the specified parent directories automatically, all of which must be otherwise empty. So `rmdir -p /one/two/three` will delete not only */one/two/three*, but also */one/two* and */one* if they exist.

File Viewing

cat	View files in their entirety
less	View files one page at a time
head	View the first lines of a file
tail	View the last lines of a file
nl	View files with their lines numbered
od	View data in octal (or other formats)
xxd	View data in hexadecimal
gv	View Postscript or PDF files
xdvi	View TeX DVI files

In Linux, you'll encounter various types of files to view: plain text, Postscript, binary data, and more. Here we'll explain how to view them. Note that commands for viewing graphics files are covered in "Graphics and Screensavers" on page 160, and audio files in "Audio and Video" on page 163.

cat [*options*] [*files*]   coreutils

/bin		stdin	stdout	- file	-- opt	--help	--version

The simplest viewer is `cat`, which just copies its files to standard output, concatenating them (hence the name). Note that large files will likely scroll off screen, so consider using `less` if you plan to view the output. That being said, `cat` is particularly useful for sending a set of files into a shell pipeline.

cat can also manipulate its output in small ways, optionally displaying nonprinting characters, prepending line numbers (though nl is more powerful for this purpose), and eliminating whitespace.

Useful options

-T	Print tabs as ^I.
-E	Print newlines as $.
-v	Print other nonprinting characters in a human-readable format.
-n	Prepend line numbers to every line.
-b	Prepend line numbers to nonblank lines.
-s	Squeeze each sequence of blank lines into a single blank line.

less [*options*] [*files*]   less

/usr/bin	stdin stdout* - file -- opt --help --version

Use less to view text one page at a time (or one window or screenful at a time). It's great for text files, or as the final command in a shell pipeline with lengthy output.

    $ command1 | command2 | command3 | command4 | less

While running less, type h for a help message describing all its features. Here are some useful keystrokes for paging through files.

Keystroke	Meaning
h, H	View a help page.
Spacebar, f, ^V, ^F	Move forward one screenful.
Enter	Move forward one line.
b, ^B, ESC-b	Move backward one screenful.
/	Enter search mode. Follow it with a regular expression and press Enter, and less will look for the first line matching it.
?	Same as /, but it searches backward in the file.
n	Repeat your most recent search forward.
N	Repeat your most recent search backward.

* Although technically less can be plugged into the middle of a pipeline, or its output redirected to a file, there isn't much point to doing this.

Keystroke	Meaning
v	Edit the current file with your default text editor (the value of environment variable VISUAL, or if not defined, EDITOR, or if not defined, vi.
<	Jump to beginning of file.
>	Jump to end of file.
:n	Jump to next file.
:p	Jump to previous file.

less has a mind-boggling number of features; we're presenting only the most common. The manpage is recommended reading.

Useful options

-c	Clear the screen before displaying the next page.
-m	Print a more verbose prompt, displaying the percentage of the file displayed so far.
-N	Prepend line numbers to the output.
-r	Display control characters literally; normally less converts them to a human-readable format.
-s	Squeeze multiple, adjacent blank lines into a single blank line.
-S	Truncate long lines to the width of the screen, instead of wrapping.

head [*options*] [*files*]   coretutils

/usr/bin	stdin	stdout	- file	-- opt	--help	--version

The head command prints the first 10 lines of a file: great for previewing the contents.

```
$ head myfile
$ head * | less          Preview all files in the current
directory
```

Useful options

-*N* -n *N*	Print the first *N* lines instead of 10.
-c *N*	Print the first *N* bytes of the file.
-q	Quiet mode: when processing more than one file, don't print a banner above each file. Normally head prints a banner containing the filename.

tail [*options*] [*files*]   coreutils

/usr/bin   stdin   stdout   - file   -- opt   --help   --version

The tail command prints the last 10 lines of a file, and does other tricks as well.

```
$ tail myfile
```

Useful options

-N -n N	Print the last N lines of the file instead of 10.
+N	Print all lines except the first N.
-c N	Print the last N bytes of the file.
-f	Keep the file open, and whenever lines are appended to the file, print them. This is extremely useful. Add the --retry option if the file doesn't exist yet, but you want to wait for it to exist.
-q	Quiet mode: when processing more than one file, don't print a banner above each file. Normally tail prints a banner containing the filename.

nl [*options*] [*files*]   coreutils

/usr/bin   stdin   stdout   - file   -- opt   --help   --version

nl copies its files to standard output, prepending line numbers. It's more flexible than cat with its -n and -b options, providing an almost bizarre amount of control over the numbering. nl can be used in two ways: on ordinary text files, and on specially marked-up text files with predefined headers and footers.

Useful options

-b [a|t|n|pR]	Prepend numbers to all lines (a), nonblank lines (t), no lines (n), or only lines that contain regular expression R. (Default=a)
-v N	Begin numbering with integer N. (Default=1)
-i N	Increment the number by N for each line, so for example, you could use odd numbers only (-i2) or even numbers only (-v2 -i2). (Default=1)
-n [ln|rn|rz]	Format numbers as left-justified (ln), right-justified (rn), or right-justified with leading zeroes (rz). (Default=ln)
-w N	Force the width of the number to be N columns. (Default=6)
-s S	Insert string S between the line number and the text. (Default=TAB)

Additionally, nl has the wacky ability to divide text files into virtual pages, each with a header, body, and footer with different numbering schemes. For this to work, however, you must insert nl-specific delimiter strings into the file: \:\:\: (start of header), \:\: (start of body), and \: (start of footer). Each must appear on a line by itself. Then you can use additional options (see the manpage) to affect line-numbering in the headers and footers of your decorated file.

od [*options*] [*files*]
coreutils

/usr/bin		stdin	stdout	- file	-- opt	--help	--version

When you want to view a binary file, consider od (Octal Dump) for the job. It copies one or more files to standard output, displaying their data in ASCII, octal, decimal, hexadecimal, or floating point, in various sizes (byte, short, long). For example, this command:

```
$ od -w8 /usr/bin/who
0000000 042577 043114 000401 000001
0000010 000000 000000 000000 000000
0000020 000002 000003 000001 000000
0000030 106240 004004 000064 000000
...
```

displays the bytes in binary file */usr/bin/who* in octal, eight bytes per line. The column on the left contains the file offset of each row, again in octal.

Useful options

-N B	Display only the first B bytes of each file, specified in decimal, hexadecimal (by prepending 0x or 0X), 512-byte blocks (by appending b), kilobytes (by appending k), or megabytes (by appending m). (Default is to display the entire file.)
-j B	Begin the output at byte B+1 of each file; acceptable formats are the same as in the -N option. (Default=0)
-w [B]	Display B bytes per line; acceptable formats are the same as in the -N option. Using -w by itself is equivalent to -w32. (Default=16)
-s [B]	Group each row of bytes into sequences of B bytes, separated by whitespace; acceptable formats are the same as in the -N option. Using -s by itself is equivalent to -s3. (Default=2)

Option	Description
-A (d|o|x|n)	Display file offsets in the leftmost column, in decimal (d), octal (o), hexadecimal (h), or not at all (n). (Default=o)
-t (a|c)[z]	Display output in a character format, with nonalphanumeric characters printed as escape sequences (a) or by name (c). For z, see below.
-t (d|o|u|x)[SIZE[z]]	Display output in an integer format, including octal (o), signed decimal (d), unsigned decimal (u), hexadecimal (x). (For binary output, use xxd instead.) SIZE represents the number of bytes per integer; it can be a positive integer or any of the values C, S, I, or L, which stand for the size of a char, short, int, or long datatype, respectively. For z, see below.
-t f[SIZE[z]]	Display output in floating point. SIZE represents the number of bytes per integer; it can be a positive integer or any of the values F, D, or L, which stand for the size of a float, double, or long double datatype, respectively. For z, see below. If -t is omitted, the default is -to2. Appending z to the -t parameter prints a new column on the right-hand side of the output, displaying the printable characters on each line, much like the default output of xxd.

xxd [*options*] [*files*]   vim-common

/usr/bin	stdin	stdout	- file	-- opt	--help	--version

Similar to od, xxd produces a hexadecimal or binary dump of a file in several different formats. It can also do the reverse, converting from its hex dump format back into the original data. For example, the command:

```
$ xxd /usr/bin/who
0000000:7f45 4c46 0101 0100 0000 0000 0000 0000  .ELF............
0000010:0200 0300 0100 0000 a08c 0408 3400 0000  ............4...
0000020:6824 0000 0000 0000 3400 2000 0600 2800  h$......4. ...(.
0000030:1900 1800 0600 0000 3400 0000 3480 0408  ........4...4...
...
```

displays a hex dump of binary file */usr/bin/who*, 16 bytes per row. The left column indicates the file offset of the row, the next eight columns contain the data, and the final column displays the printable characters in the row, if any.

xxd produces three-column output by default: file offsets, the data in hex, and the data as text (printable characters only).

Useful options

-l *N*	Display only the first *N* bytes. (Default is to display the entire file)
-s *N* -s -*N*	Begin at a position other than the first byte of the file. The first form skips the first *N* bytes. The second (-*N*) begins *N* bytes from the end of the file. (There is also a +*N* syntax for more advanced skipping through standard input; see the manpage.)
-c *N*	Display *N* bytes per row. (Default=16)
-g *N*	Group each row of bytes into sequences of *N* bytes, separated by whitespace, like od -s. (Default=2)
-b	Display the output in binary instead of hexadecimal.
-u	Display the output in uppercase hexadecimal instead of lowercase.
-p	Display the output as a plain hexdump, 60 contiguous bytes per line.
-i	Display the output as a C programming language data structure. When reading from a file, it produces an array of unsigned chars containing the data, and an unsigned int containing the array length. When reading from standard input, it produces only a comma-separated list of hex bytes.
-r	The reverse operation: convert from an xxd hex dump back into the original file format. Works with the default hexdump format and, if you add the -p option, the plain hexdump format. If you're bored, try either of these commands to convert and unconvert a file in a pipeline, reproducing the original file on standard output: `$ xxd myfile	xxd -r` `$ xxd -p myfile	xxd -r -p`

gv [*options*] *file*   gv

/usr/X11R6/bin   stdin   stdout   - file   -- opt   --help   --version

GhostView displays an Adobe Postscript or PDF file in an X window. You can invoke it as gv or ghostview. The basic operation of the program is simple: click the desired page number to jump to that page, and so forth. A few minutes of playing time and you'll have the hang of it.

GhostView is the definitive Linux Postscript viewer, but other free PDF viewers include acroread (*http://www.adobe.com/*) and xpdf (*http://www.foolabs.com/xpdf/*).

Useful options

`-page` *P*	Begin on page *P*. (Default=1)

`-monochrome`
`-grayscale`
`-color`
	Use the given display mode.

`-portrait`
`-landscape`
`-seascape`
`-upsidedown`
	Choose the page orientation, which normally gv determines automatically.

`-scale` *N*	Set the scaling factor (i.e., the zoom) for the display. The integer *N* may be positive (make the image larger) or negative (smaller).
`-watch` `-nowatch`	Automatically reload the Postscript file (or don't) when it changes.

xdvi [*options*] *file*

tetex-xdvi

/usr/bin   stdin   stdout   - file   -- opt   --help   --version

The document processing system TeX produces binary output files in a format called DVI, with suffix *.dvi*. The viewer xdvi displays a DVI file in an X window. If you prefer, convert a DVI file to Postscript via the dvips command and then use GhostView (gv) to display it:

```
$ dvips -o myfile.ps myfile.dvi
$ gv myfile.ps
```

While displaying a file, xdvi has a column of buttons down the right-hand side with obvious uses, such as Next to move to the next page. (You can hide the buttons by invoking xdvi with the -expert option.) You can also navigate the file by keystroke.

Keystroke	Meaning
q	Quit.
n, Spacebar, Enter, Pagedown	Jump to next page. Precede it with a number *N* to jump by *N* pages..
p, Backspace, Delete, Pageup	Jump to previous page. Precede it with a number *N* to jump by *N* pages.
<	Jump to first page.
>	Jump to last page.

Keystroke	Meaning
^L	Redisplay the page.
R	Reread the DVI file, say, after you've modified it.
Press mouse buttons	Magnify a rectangular region under the mouse cursor.

xdvi has dozens of command-line options for tailoring its colors, geometry, zoom, and overall behavior.

File Creation and Editing

emacs	Text editor from Free Software Foundation
vim	Text editor, extension of Unix vi
umask	Set a default mode for new files and directories
soffice	Office suite for editing Microsoft Word, Excel, and PowerPoint documents
abiword	Edit Microsoft Word documents
gnumeric	Edit Excel spreadsheets

To get far with Linux, you must become proficient with one of its text editors. The two major ones are emacs from the Free Software Foundation, and vim, a successor to the Unix editor vi. Teaching these editors fully is beyond the scope of this book, but both have online tutorials, and we list common operations in Table 1. To edit a file, run either:

```
$ emacs myfile
$ vim myfile
```

If *myfile* doesn't exist, it is created automatically. You can also quickly create an empty file (for later editing) using the touch command (see "File Properties" on page 56):

```
$ touch newfile
```

or write data into a new file by redirecting the output of a program (see "Input/output redirection" on page 26):

```
$ echo anything at all > newfile
```

In case you share files with Microsoft Windows systems, we will also cover Linux programs that edit Microsoft Word, Excel, and PowerPoint documents.

Your Default Editor

Various Linux programs will run an editor when necessary, and by default the editor is vim. For example, your email program may invoke an editor to compose a new message, and less invokes an editor if you type "v". But what if you don't want vim to be your default editor? Set the environment variables VISUAL and EDITOR to your choice, for example:

```
$ EDITOR=emacs
$ VISUAL=emacs
$ export EDITOR VISUAL          Optional
```

Both variables are necessary because different programs check one variable or the other. Set EDITOR and VISUAL in your ~/.bash_profile startup file if you want your choices made permanent. Any program can be made your default editor as long as it accepts a filename as an argument.

Regardless of how you set these variables, all system administrators should know at least basic vim and emacs commands in case a system tool suddenly runs an editor on a critical file.

emacs [*options*] [*files*]   emacs

/usr/bin		stdin	stdout	- file	-- opt	--help	--version

emacs is an extremely powerful editing environment with more commands than you could possibly imagine, and a complete programming language built in to define your own editing features. To invoke the emacs tutorial, run:

```
$ emacs
```

and type ^h t.

Most emacs keystroke commands involve the control key (like ^F) or the *meta* key, which is usually the Escape key or the Alt key. emacs's own documentation notates the meta key as M- (as in M-F to mean "hold the meta key and type F") so we will too. For basic keystrokes, see Table 1.

vim [*options*] [*files*]

vim-enhanced

/usr/bin		stdin	stdout	- file	-- opt	--help	--version

vim is an enhanced version of the old standard Unix editor vi. To run the vim tutorial, run:

```
$ vimtutor
```

vim is a mode-based editor. It operates in two modes, *insert* and *normal*. Insert mode is for entering text in the usual manner, while normal mode is for running commands like "delete a line" or copy/paste. For basic keystrokes in normal mode, see Table 1.

Table 1. Basic keystrokes in emacs and vim

Task	emacs	vim
Run editor in current window	$ emacs -nw [*file*]	$ vim [*file*]
Run Editor in a new X window	$ emacs [*file*]	$ gvim [*file*]
Type text	*text*	i *text* ESC
Save & quit	^x^s then ^x^c	:wq
Quit without saving	^x^c Respond "no" when asked to save buffers	:q!
Save	^x^s	:w
Save As	^x^w	:w *filename*
Undo	^_	u
Suspend editor (not in X)	^z	^z
Switch to edit mode	(*N/A*)	ESC
Switch to command mode	M-x	:
Abort command in progress	^g	ESC
Move forward	^f or right arrow	l or right arrow
Move backward	^b or left arrow	h or left arrow
Move up	^p or up arrow	k or up arrow
Move down	^n or down arrow	j or down arrow
Move to next word	M-f	w

Table 1. Basic keystrokes in emacs and vim (continued)

Task	emacs	vim
Move to previous word	M-b	b
Move to beginning of line	^a	0
Move to end of line	^e	$
Move down 1 screen	^v	^f
Move up 1 screen	M-v	^b
Move to beginning of buffer	M-<	gg
Move to end of buffer	M->	G
Delete next character	^d	x
Delete previous character	BACKSPACE	X
Delete next word	M-d	de
Delete previous word	M-BACKSPACE	db
Delete current line	^a^k^k	dd
Delete to end of line	^k	d$
Define region (type this keystroke to mark the beginning of the region, then move the cursor to the end of the desired region)	^Spacebar	v
Cut region	^w	d
Copy region	M-w	y
Paste region	^y	p
Get help	^h	:help
Get user manual	^h i	:help

umask [*options*] [*mask*]   bash

shell built-in   stdin   **stdout**   - file   -- opt   --help   --version

The umask command sets or prints your default mode for creating files and directories: whether they are readable, writable, and/or executable by yourself, your group, and the world. (See "File Protections" on page 19, and the chmod command in "File Properties" on page 56, for more information.)

```
$ umask
0002
```

```
$ umask -S
u=rwx,g=rwx,o=rx
```

First, some technical talk. A umask value is a *mask*, i.e., a binary value that is combined (using the binary XOR operation) with 0666 for files and 0777 for directories) to produce your default protection mode. For example, 0002 XOR 0666 yields 0664 for files, and 0002 XOR 0777 yields mode 0775 for directories.

If that explanation seems from outer space, here is a simple recipe. Use mask 0022 to give yourself full privileges, and all others read/execute privileges only:

```
$ umask 0022
$ touch newfile && mkdir dir
$ ls -ld newfile dir
-rw-r--r--  1 smith smith     0 Nov 11 12:25 newfile
drwxr-xr-x  2 smith smith  4096 Nov 11 12:25 dir
```

Use mask 0002 to give yourself and your default group full privileges, and read/execute to others:

```
$ umask 0002
$ touch newfile && mkdir dir
$ ls -ld newfile dir
-rw-rw-r--  1 smith smith     0 Nov 11 12:26 newfile
drwxrwxr-x  2 smith smith  4096 Nov 11 12:26 dir
```

Use mask 0077 to give yourself full privileges with nothing for anyone else:

```
$ umask 0077
$ touch newfile && mkdir dir
$ ls -ld newfile dir
-rw-------  1 smith smith     0 Nov 11 12:27 newfile
drwx------  2 smith smith  4096 Nov 11 12:27 dir
```

soffice [*files*]   openoffice.org

/usr/lib/openoffice/programs	stdin	stdout	- file	-- opt	--help	--version

OpenOffice.org[*] is a comprehensive, integrated office software suite that can edit Microsoft Word, Excel, and PowerPoint files. Simply run:

```
$ soffice
```

---

[*] The ".org" is part of the software package's name.

and you're ready to work. The same program edits all three types of files.* It is a large program that requires plenty of memory and disk space.

OpenOffice.org can also handle drawings (sdraw command), faxes (sfax), mailing labels (slabel), and more. *http://www.openoffice.org/* has more information, or you can use the soffice Help menu.

abiword [*options*] [*files*]   abiword

/usr/bin		stdin	stdout	- file	-- opt	--help	--version

abiword is another program for editing Microsoft Word documents. It is smaller and quicker than soffice, though not as powerful, and perfectly suitable for many editing tasks. If you specify files on the command line, they must exist: abiword won't create them for you.

gnumeric [*options*] [*files*]   gnumeric

/usr/bin		stdin	stdout	- file	-- opt	--help	--version

gnumeric is a spreadsheet program that can edit Microsoft Excel documents. It is quite powerful and fast, and if you've used Excel before, gnumeric will feel familiar. If you specify files on the command line, they must exist: gnumeric won't create them for you.

File Properties

stat	Display attributes of files and directories
wc	Count bytes, words, lines in a file
du	Measure disk usage of files and directories
file	Identify (guess) the type of a file
touch	Change timestamps of files and directories

---

* Under the hood, soffice comprises the separate programs Writer (swriter command) for word processing, Calc (scalc) for spreadsheets, and Impress (simpress) for presentations, which you can run directly if desired.

---

chown	Change owner of files and directories
chgrp	Change group ownership of files and directories
chmod	Change protection mode of files and directories
chattr	Change extended attributes of files and directories
lsattr	List extended attributes of files and directories

When examining a Linux file, the contents are only half the story. Every file and directory also has attributes that describe its owner, size, access permissions, and other information. The ls -l command (see "Basic File Operations" on page 37) displays some of these attributes, but other commands provide additional information.

stat [*options*] *files* coreutils

usr/bin		stdin	stdout	- file	-- opt	--help	--version

The stat command lists important attributes of files (by default) or filesystems (-f option). File information looks like:

```
$ stat myfile
  File: "myfile"
  Size: 1264      Blocks: 8          Regular File
Access: (0644/-rw-r--r--)      Uid: ( 600/smith)  Gid:
( 620/users)
Device: 30a      Inode: 99492       Links: 1
Access: Fri Aug 29 00:16:12 2003
Modify: Wed Jul 23 23:09:41 2003
Change: Wed Jul 23 23:11:48 2003
```

and includes the filename, size in bytes (1264), size in blocks (8), file type (Regular File), permissions in octal (0644), permissions in the format of "ls -l" (-rw-r--r--), owner's user ID (600), owner's name (smith), owner's group ID (620), owner's group name (users), device type (30a), inode number (99492), number of hard links (1), and timestamps of the file's most recent access, modification, and status change. Filesystem information looks like:

```
$ stat -f myfile
  File: "myfile"
    ID: bffff358 ffffffff Namelen: 255      Type: EXT2
Blocks: Total: 2016068    Free: 876122      Available:
773709      Size: 4096
Inodes: Total: 1026144    Free: 912372
```

and includes the filename (*myfile*), filesystem ID (bffff358 ffffffff), maximum length of a filename for that filesystem (255 bytes), filesystem type (EXT2), the counts of total, free, and available blocks in the filesystem (2016068, 876122, and 773709, respectively), block size for the filesystem (4096), and the counts of total and free inodes (1026144 and 912372, respectively).

The -t option presents the same data but on a single line, without headings. This is handy for processing by shell scripts or other programs.

```
$ stat -t myfile
myfile 1264 8 81a4 500 500 30a 99492 1 44 1e 1062130572
1059016181 1059016308
$ stat -tf myfile
myfile bffff358 ffffffff 255 ef53 2016068 875984 773571
4096 1026144 912372
```

Useful options

-l   Follow symbolic links and report on the file they point to.

-f   Report on the filesystem containing the file, not the file itself.

-t   Terse mode: print information on a single line.

wc [*options*] [*files*]   coreutils

/usr/bin		stdin	stdout	- file	-- opt	--help	--version

The wc (word count) program prints a count of bytes, words, and lines in (presumably) a text file.

```
$ wc myfile
    24      62      428 myfile
```

This file has 24 lines, 62 whitespace-delimited words, and 428 bytes.

Useful options

-l   Print the line count only.

-w   Print the word count only.

-c   Print the byte (character) count only.

-L   Locate the longest line in each file and print its length in bytes.

du [*options*] [*files* | *directories*]
coreutils

/usr/bin   stdin   stdout   - file   -- opt   --help   --version

The du (disk usage) command measures the disk space occupied by files or directories. By default, it measures the current directory and all its subdirectories, printing totals in blocks for each, with a grand total at the bottom.

```
$ du
8     ./Notes
36    ./Mail
340   ./Files/mine
40    ./Files/bob
416   ./Files
216   ./PC
2404  .
```

However, it can also measure the size of files:

```
$ du myfile myfile2
4     ./myfile
16    ./myfile2
```

Useful options

-b -k -m   Measure usage in bytes (-b), kilobytes (-k), or megabytes (-m).

-B *N*   Display sizes in blocks that you define, where 1 block = *N* bytes. (Default = 1024)

-h -H   Print "human readable" output, and choose the most appropriate unit for each size. For example, if two directories are of size 1 gigabyte or 25 kilobytes, respectively, du -h prints 1G and 25K. The -h option uses powers of 1024 whereas -H uses powers of 1000.

-c   Print a total in the last line. This is the default behavior when measuring a directory, but for measuring individual files, provide -c if you want a total.

-L   Follow symbolic links and measure the files they point to.

-s   Print only the total size.

file [*options*] *files*
file

/usr/bin   stdin   stdout   - file   -- opt   --help   --version

The file command reports the type of a file:

```
$ file /etc/hosts /usr/bin/who letter.doc
/etc/hosts:    ASCII text
```

```
/usr/bin/who:   ELF 32-bit LSB executable, Intel 80386 ...
letter.doc:     Microsoft Office Document
```

Unlike some other operating systems, Linux does not keep track of file types, so the output is an educated guess based on the file content and other factors.

Useful options

-b	Omit filenames (left column of output).
-i	Print MIME types for the file, such as "text/plain" or "audio/mpeg", instead of the usual output.
-f *name_file*	Read filenames, one per line, from the given *name_file* (and report their types), and afterward process filenames on the command line as usual.
-L	Follow symbolic links, reporting the type of the destination file instead of the link.
-z	If a file is compressed (see "File Compression and Packaging" on page 82), examine the uncompressed contents to decide the file type, instead of reporting "compressed data."

touch [*options*] *files*   coreutils

/bin		stdin	stdout	- file	-- opt	--help	--version

The touch command changes two timestamps associated with a file: its modification time (when the file's data was last changed) and its access time (when the file was last read).

```
$ touch myfile
```

You can set these timestamps to arbitrary values, e.g.:

```
$ touch -d "November 18 1975" myfile
```

If a given file doesn't exist, touch creates it, a handy way to create empty files.

Useful options

-a	Change the access time only.
-m	Change the modification time only.
-c	If the file doesn't exist, don't create it (normally, touch creates it).

-d *timestamp*   Set the file's timestamp(s). A tremendous number of timestamp formats are acceptable, from "12/28/2001 3pm" to "28-May" (the current year is assumed, and a time of midnight) to "next tuesday 13:59" to "0" (midnight today). Experiment and check your work with `stat`. Full documentation is available from `info touch`.

-t *timestamp*   A less intelligent way to set the file's *timestamp*, using the format [[*CC*]*YY*]*MMDDhhmm*[.*ss*], where *CC* is the two-digit century, *YY* is the two-digit year, *MM* is the 2-digit month, *DD* is the two-digit day, *hh* is the two-digit hour, *mm* is the two-digit minute, and *ss* is the two-digit second. For example, `-t 20030812150047` represents August 12, 2003, at 15:00:47.

chown [*options*] *user_spec files*   coreutils

/bin	stdin	stdout	- file	-- opt	--help	--version

The chown (change owner) command sets the ownership of files and directories.

    $ chown smith myfile myfile2 mydir

The *user_spec* parameter may be any of these possibilities:

- A username (or numeric user ID), to set the owner
- A username (or numeric user ID), optionally followed by a colon and a group name (or numeric group ID), to set the owner and group
- A username (or numeric user ID) followed by a colon, to set the owner *and* to set the group to the invoking user's login group
- A group name (or numeric group ID) preceded by a colon, to set the group only
- --reference=*file* to set the same owner and group as another given file

Useful options

--dereference   Follow symbolic links and operate on the files they point to.

-R   Recursively change the ownership within a directory hierarchy.

chgrp [*options*] *group_spec files* coreutils

The chgrp (change group) command sets the group ownership of files and directories.

```
$ chgrp smith myfile myfile2 mydir
```

The *group_spec* parameter may be any of these possibilities:

- A group name or numeric group ID
- --reference=*file*, to set the same group ownership as another given file

See "Working with Groups" on page 119 for more information on groups.

Useful options

--dereference	Follow symbolic links and operate on the files they point to.
-R	Recursively change the ownership within a directory hierarchy.

chmod [*options*] *permissions files* coreutils

The chmod (change mode) command sets access permissions for files and directories. Not every file should be available to everyone (this isn't Windows 95, y'know), and chmod is the tool for ensuring this. Typical permissions are read, write, and execute, and they may be limited to the file owner, the file's group owner, and/or other users. The permissions argument can take three different forms:

- --reference=*file*, to set the same permissions as another given file
- An octal number, up to four digits long, that specifies the file's *absolute* permissions in bits. The leftmost digit is special (described later) and the second, third, and fourth represent the file's owner, the file's group, and all users. See Figure 3 for an example, displaying the meaning of mode 0640.
- One or more strings specifying *absolute or relative* permissions (i.e., relative to the file's existing permissions) to be applied, separated by commas.

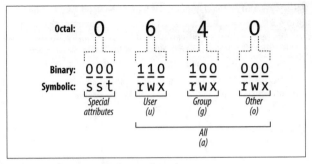

Figure 3. File permission bits explained

In the third form, each string consists of three parts: an optional *scope*, a *command*, and *permissions*.

Scope (optional)
> u for user, g for group, o for other users not in the group, a for all users. The default is a.

Command
> + to add permissions, - to remove permissions, = to set absolute permissions, ignoring existing ones

Permissions
> r for read, w for write/modify, x for execute (for directories, this is permission to cd into the directory), X for conditional execute (explained later), u to duplicate the user permissions, g to duplicate the group permissions, o to duplicate the "other users" permissions, s for setuid or setgid, and t for the sticky bit.

For example, ug+rw would add read and write permission for the user and the group, a-x (or just -x) would remove execute permission for everyone, and u=r would first remove all existing permissions and then make the file readable only by its owner. You can combine these strings by separating them with commas, such as ug+rw,a-x.

Setuid and setgid apply to executable files (programs and scripts). Suppose we have an executable file *F* owned by user "smith" and the group "friends". If file *F* has setuid (set user ID) enabled, then anyone who runs *F* will "become" user smith, with all her rights and privileges, for the duration of the program. Likewise, if *F* has setgid (set group ID) enabled, anyone who executes *F* becomes a member of the friends group for the duration of the program. As you might imagine, setuid and setgid can impact system security, so don't use them unless you *really* know what you're doing. One misplaced chmod +s can leave your whole system vulnerable to attack.

Conditional execute permission (X) means the same as x, except that it succeeds only if the file is already executable, or if the file is a directory. Otherwise it has no effect.

Useful options

-R   Recursively change the ownership within a directory hierarchy.

chattr [*options*] [+ −=]*attributes* [*files*]   e2fsprogs

/usr/bin		stdin	stdout	- file	-- opt	--help	--version

If you grew up with other Unix systems, you might be surprised that Linux files can have additional attributes beyond their access permissions. If a file is on an ext2 or ext3 filesystem (the Fedora default), you can set these extended attributes with the chattr (change attribute) command and list them with lsattr.

As with chmod, attributes may be added (+) or removed (-) relatively, or set absolutely (=).

Attribute	Meaning
a	Append-only: appends are permitted to this file, but it cannot otherwise be edited. Root only.
A	Accesses not timestamped: accesses to this file don't update its access timestamp (atime).
c	Compressed: data is transparently compressed on writes and uncompressed on reads.
d	Don't dump: tell the dump program to ignore this file when making backups (see "Backups and Remote Storage" on page 95).
i	Immutable: file cannot be changed or deleted (root only).
j	Journaled data (ext3 filesystems only).
s	Secure deletion: if deleted, this file's data is overwritten with zeroes.
S	Synchronous update: changes are written to disk immediately, as if you had typed sync after saving (see "Disks and Filesystems" on page 91).
u	Undeletable: file cannot be deleted (undeletable).

Useful options

-R   Recursively process directories.

lsattr [*options*] [*files*]

e2fsprogs

/usr/bin   stdin   **stdout**   - file   -- opt   --**help**   --version

If you set extended attributes with chattr, you can view them with lsattr (list attributes). The output uses the same letters as chattr; for example, this file is immutable and undeletable:

```
$ lsattr myfile
-u--i--- myfile
```

Useful options

-R   Recursively process directories.

-a   List all files, including those whose names begin with a dot.

-d   If listing a directory, do not list its contents, just the directory itself.

With no files specified, lsattr prints the attributes of all files in the current directory.

File Location

find	Locate files in a directory hierarchy
slocate	Create an index of files, and search the index for string
which	Locate executables in your search path (command)
type	Locate executables in your search path (bash builtin)
whereis	Locate executables, documentation, and source files

Linux systems can contain tens or hundreds of thousands of files easily. How can you find a particular file when you need to? The first step is to organize your files logically into directories in some thoughtful manner, but there are several other ways to find files, depending what you're looking for.

For finding any file, find is a brute-force program that slogs file-by-file through a directory hierarchy to locate a target. slocate is much faster, searching through a prebuilt index that you generate as needed. (Fedora generates the index nightly by default.)

For finding programs, the which and type commands check all directories in your shell search path. type is built into the bash shell (and therefore available only when running bash), while which is a program (normally */usr/bin/which*); type is faster and can detect shell aliases.* In contrast, whereis examines a known set of directories, rather than your search path.

find [*directories*] [*expression*]   findutils

/usr/bin		stdin	**stdout**	- file	-- opt	--help	--version

The find command searches one or more directories (and their subdirectories recursively) for files matching certain criteria. It is very powerful, with over 50 options and, unfortunately, a rather unusual syntax. Here are some simple examples that search the entire file system from the root directory:

Find a particular file named *myfile*:

    $ find / -type f -name myfile -print

Print all directory names:

    $ find / -type d -print

Useful options

-name *pattern* -path *pattern* -lname *pattern* -iname *pattern* -ipath *pattern* -ilname *pattern*	The name (-name), pathname (-path), or symbolic link target (-lname) of the desired file must match this shell pattern, which may include shell wildcards *, ?, and []. Paths are relative to the directory tree being searched. The -iname, -ipath and -ilname options are the same as -name, -path, and -lname, respectively, but are case-insensitive.
-regex *regexp*	The path (relative to the directory tree being searched) must match the given regular expression.

---

* The tcsh shell performs some trickery to make which detect aliases.

-type f|d|l|b|c|p|s	Locate only plain files (f), directories (d), symbolic links (l), block devices (b), character devices (c), named pipes (p), or sockets (s).
-atime N -ctime N -mtime N	File was last accessed (-atime), last modified (-mtime), or had a status change (-ctime) exactly $N*24$ hours ago. Use $+N$ for "greater than N," or $-N$ for "less than N."
-amin N -cmin N -mmin N	File was last accessed (-amin), last modified (-mmin), or had a status change (-cmin) exactly N minutes ago. Use $+N$ for "greater than N," or $-N$ for "less than N."
-anewer other_file -cnewer other_file -newer other_file	File was accessed (-anewer), modified (-newer), or had a status change (-cnewer) more recently than other_file has.
-maxdepth N -mindepth N	Consider files at least (-mindepth) or at most (-maxdepth) N levels deep in the directory tree being searched.
-follow	Dereference symbolic links.
-depth	Proceed using depth-first search: completely search a directory's contents (recursively) before operating on the directory itself.
-xdev	Limit the search to a single filesystem, i.e., don't cross device boundaries.
-size N[bckw]	Consider files of size N, which can be given in blocks (b), one-byte characters (c), kilobytes (k), or two-byte words (w). Use $+N$ for "greater than N," or $-N$ for "less than N."
-empty	File has zero size, and is a regular file or directory.
-user name -group name	File is owned by the given username or group name.
-perm mode -perm -mode -perm +mode	File has permissions equal to mode. Use -mode to check that *all* of the given bits are set, or +mode to check that *any* of the given bits are set.

You can group and negate parts of the expression with the following operators:

expression1 -a expression2

> And. (This is the default if two expressions appear side by side, so the "-a" is optional.)

expression1 -o expression2

> Or.

! expression
-not expression
> Negate the expression

(expression)
> Precedence markers, just like in algebra class. Evaluate what's in parentheses first. You may need to escape these from the shell with "\".

expression1 , expression2
> Same as the comma operator in the C programming language. Evaluate both expressions and return the value of the second one.

Once you've specified the search criteria, you can tell find to perform these actions on files that match the criteria.

Useful options

-print	Simply print the path to the file, relative to the search directory.
-printf *string*	Print the given string, which may have substitutions applied to it in the manner of the C library function, printf( ). See the manpage for the full list of outputs.
-print0	Like -print, but instead of separating each line of output with a newline character, use a null (ASCII 0) character. Use this when you are piping the output of find to another program, and your list of filenames may contain space characters. Of course, the receiving program must be capable of reading and parsing these null-separated lines—for example, xargs -0.
-exec *cmd* ; -ok *cmd* ;	Invoke the given shell command, *cmd*. Make sure to escape any shell metacharacters, including the required, final semicolon, so they are not immediately evaluated on the command line. Also, the symbol "{}" (make sure to quote or escape it) represents the path to the file found. The -ok action prompts the user before invoking the shell command; -exec does not.
-ls	Perform ls -dils on the file.

find, which produces a list of files on standard output, makes a great partner with xargs, which reads a list of files on standard input and applies a command to them (see man xargs). For example, to search your current directory hierarchy for files containing the word "myxomatosis":

```
$ find . -print0 | xargs -0 grep myxomatosis
```

The slocate (secure locate) command creates an index (database) of file locations and searches it quickly. If you plan to locate many files over time in a directory hierarchy that doesn't change much, slocate is a good choice. For locating a single file or performing more complex processing of found files, use find.

Fedora Linux automatically indexes the entire filesystem once a day, but if you ever need to create an index yourself (say, storing it in */tmp/myindex*), run:

```
$ slocate -u -o /tmp/myindex
```

To create an index of a given directory and all its subdirectories:

```
$ slocate -U directory -o /tmp/myindex
```

Then to search for a string in the index:

```
$ slocate -d /tmp/myindex string
```

What makes slocate "secure?" During searches, it will not display files that you ordinarily would not have permission to see. So if the superuser created an index of a protected directory, a non-superuser could search it but not see the protected files.

Indexing options

-u	Create index from the root directory downward.
-U *directory*	Create index from *directory* downward.
-l (0|1)	Turn security off (0) or on (1). The default is 1.
-e *directories*	Exclude one or more directories from the index. Separate their paths by commas.
-o *outfile*	Write the index to file *outfile*.

Search options

-d *index*	Indicate which index to use (in our example, */tmp/myindex*).
-i	Case-insensitive search.
-r *regexp*	Search for files matching the given regular expression.

which *file* which

/usr/bin		stdin	**stdout**	- file	-- opt	--help	--version

The which command locates an executable file in your shell's search path. If you've been invoking a program by typing its name:

```
$ who
```

the which command tells you where this command is located:

```
$ which who
/usr/bin/who
```

You can even find the which program itself:

```
$ which which
/usr/bin/which
```

If several programs in your search path have the same name (say, */usr/bin/who* and */usr/local/bin/who*), which reports only the first.

type [*options*] *commands* bash

shell built-in		stdin	**stdout**	- file	-- opt	--help	--version

The type command, like which, locates an executable file in your shell's search path:

```
$ type grep who
grep is /bin/grep
who is /usr/bin/who
```

However, type is built into the bash shell, whereas which is a program on disk:

```
$ type which type rm if
which is /usr/bin/which
type is a shell builtin
rm is aliased to `/bin/rm -i'
if is a shell keyword
```

As a built-in command, type is faster than which; however, it's available only if you're running bash.

whereis [*options*] *files* util-linux

/usr/bin		stdin	**stdout**	- file	-- opt	--help	--version

The whereis command attempts to locate the given files by searching a hardcoded list of directories. It can find executables, documentation, and source code. whereis is somewhat quirky because its list of directories might not include the ones you need.

Useful options

-b -m -s	List only executables (-b), manpages (-m), or source code files (-s).
-B *dirs*... -f *files*... -M *dirs*... -f *files*... -S *dirs*... -f *files*...	Search for executables (-B), manpages (-M), or source code files (-S) only in the given directories. You must terminate the directory list with the -f option before listing the files you seek.

File Text Manipulation

grep	Find lines in a file that match a regular expression
cut	Extract columns from a file
paste	Append columns
tr	Translate characters into other characters
sort	Sort lines of text by various criteria
uniq	Locate identical lines in a file
tee	Copy a file *and* print it on standard output, simultaneously

One of Linux's greatest strengths is text manipulation: massaging a text file (or standard input) into a desired form by applying transformations. Any program that reads standard input and writes standard output falls into this category, but here we'll present some of the most common and powerful.

grep [*options*] *pattern* [*files*]   grep

/bin	stdin	stdout	- file	-- opt	--help	--version

The grep command is one of the most consistently useful and powerful in the Linux arsenal. Its premise is simple: given one or more files, print all lines in those files that match a particular regular expression pattern. For example, if a file contains these lines:

```
The quick brown fox jumped over the lazy dogs!
My very eager mother just served us nine pancakes.
Film at eleven.
```

and we search for all lines containing "pancake", we get:

```
$ grep pancake myfile
My very eager mother just served us nine pancakes.
```

grep can use two different types of regular expressions, which it calls *basic* and *extended*. They are equally powerful, just different, and you may prefer one over the other based on your experience with other grep implementations. The basic syntax is in Table 2 and Table 3.

Useful options

-v	Print only lines that *do not* match the regular expression.
-l	Print only the *names* of files that contain matching lines, not the lines themselves.
-L	Print only the names of files that *do not* contain matching lines.
-c	Print only a count of matching lines.
-n	In front of each line of matching output, print its original line number.
-b	In front of each line of matching output, print the byte offset of the line in the input file.
-i	Case-insensitive match.
-w	Match only complete words (i.e., words that match the entire regular expression).
-x	Match only complete lines (i.e., lines that match the entire regular expression). Overrides -w.
-A *N*	After each matching line, print the next *N* lines from its file.
-B *N*	Before each matching line, print the previous *N* lines from its file.
-C *N*	Same as -A *N* -B *N*: print *N* lines (from the original file) above *and* below each matching line.
-r	Recursively search all files in a directory and its subdirectories.
-E	Use extended regular expressions. See egrep.
-F	Use lists of fixed strings instead of regular expressions. See fgrep.

egrep [*options*] *pattern* [*files*]

grep

/bin   stdin   stdout   - file   -- opt   --help   --version

The egrep command is just like grep, but uses a different
("extended") language for regular expressions. It's the same as
grep -E.

Table 2. Plain and extended regular expressions for grep

Regular expression	Meaning
.	Any single character.
[...]	Match any single character in this list.
[^...]	Match any single character NOT in this list.
(...)	Grouping.
^	Beginning of a line.
$	End of a line.
\<	Beginning of a word.
\>	End of a word.
[:alnum:]	Any alphanumeric character.
[:alpha:]	Any alphabetic character.
[:cntrl:]	Any control character.
[:digit:]	Any digit.
[:graph:]	Any graphic character.
[:lower:]	Any lowercase letter.
[:print:]	Any printable character.
[:punct:]	Any punctuation mark.
[:space:]	Any whitespace character.
[:upper:]	Any uppercase letter.
[:xdigit:]	Any hexadecimal digit.
*	Zero or more repetitions of a regular expression.
\c	The character *c* literally, even if *c* is a special regular expression character. For example, use * to match an asterisk or \\ to match a backslash. Alternatively, put the literal character inside square brackets, like [*] or [\].

Table 3. Differences: plain and extended regular expressions

Plain	Extended	Meaning
|	|	Or.
\+	+	One or more repetitions of a regular expression.
\?	?	Zero or one occurrence of a regular expression.
\{n\}	{n}	Exactly *n* repetitions of a regular expression.
\{n,\}	{n,}	*n* or more repetitions of a regular expression.
\{n,m\}	{n,m}	Between *n* and *m* (inclusive) repetitions of a regular expression, *n* < *m*.

fgrep [*options*] [*fixed_strings*] [*files*]   grep

/bin		stdin	stdout	- file	-- opt	--help	--version

The fgrep command is just like grep, but instead of accepting a regular expression, it accepts a list of fixed strings, separated by newlines. It's the same as grep -F. For example, to search for the strings one, two, and three in a file:

```
$ fgrep 'one          Note we are typing newline characters
two
three' myfile
```

fgrep is commonly used with the lowercase -f option, which reads patterns from a file. For example, if you have a dictionary file full of strings, one per line:

```
$ cat my_dictionary_file
aardvark
aback
abandon
...
```

you can conveniently search for those strings in a set of input files:

```
$ fgrep -f my_dictionary_file *
```

fgrep also is good for searching for nonalphanumeric characters like * and { because they are taken literally, not as metacharacters in regular expressions.

cut -(b|c|f)*range* [*options*] [*files*]   coreutils

/usr/bin   stdin   stdout   - file   -- opt   --help   --version

The cut command extracts columns of text from files. A "column"
is defined either by character offsets (e.g., the nineteenth character of each line):

```
$ cut -c19 myfile
```

by byte offsets (which are often the same as characters, unless you
have multibyte characters in your language):

```
$ cut -b19 myfile
```

or by delimited fields (e.g., the fifth field in each line of a comma-
delimited file):

```
$ cut -d, -f5 myfile
```

You aren't limited to printing a single column: you can provide a
range (3–16), a comma-separated sequence (3,4,5,6,8,16), or both
(3,4,8-16). For ranges, if you omit the first number (–16), a 1 is
assumed (1–16); if you omit the last number (5–), the end of line
is used.

Useful options

-d *C*	Use character *C* as the *input* delimiter character between fields for - f. By default it's a tab character.
--output-delimiter=*C*	Use character *C* as the *output* delimiter character between fields for - f. By default it's a tab character.
-s	Suppress (don't print) lines that don't contain the delimiter character.

paste [*options*] [*files*]   coreutils

/usr/bin   stdin   stdout   - file   -- opt   --help   --version

The paste command is the opposite of cut: treat several files as
vertical columns and combine them on standard output:

```
$ cat letters
A
B
C
$ cat numbers
1
2
3
```

```
4
5
$ paste numbers letters
1    A
2    B
3    C
4
5
$ paste letters numbers
A    1
B    2
C    3
     4
     5
```

Useful options

-d *delimiters*   Use the given *delimiters* characters between columns; the default
                  is a tab character. You can provide a single character (-d:) to be used
                  always, or a list of characters (-dxyz) to be applied in sequence on
                  each line (the first delimiter is x, then y, then z, then x, then y, ...).

-s   Transpose the rows and columns of output:
```
$ paste -s letters numbers
A    B    C
1    2    3    4    5
```

tr [*options*] *charset1* [*charset2*]   coreutils

/usr/bin	stdin	stdout	- file	-- opt	--help	--version

The tr command performs some simple, useful translations of one
set of characters into another. For example, to change all vowels
into asterisks:

```
$ cat myfile
This is a very wonderful file.
$ cat myfile | tr aeiouAEIOU '*'
Th*s *s * v*ry w*nd*rf*l f*l*.
```

or to delete all vowels:

```
$ cat myfile | tr -d aeiouAEIOU
Ths s  vry wndrfl fl.
```

or to capitalize everything in the file:

```
$ cat myfile | tr 'a-z' 'A-Z'
THIS IS A VERY WONDERFUL FILE.
```

tr translates the first character in *charset1* into the first character in *charset2*, the second into the second, the third into the third, etc. If the length of *charset1* is *N*, only the first *N* characters in *charset2* are used. (If *charset1* is longer than *charset2*, see the -t option.)

Character sets can have the following forms.

Form	Meaning
ABCD	The sequence of characters A, B, C, D.
A-B	The range of characters from A to B.
[x*y]	y repetitions of the character x.
[:class:]	The same character classes ([:alnum:], [:digit:], etc.) accepted by grep.

tr also understands the escape characters "\a" (^G = ring bell), "\b" (^H = backspace), "\f" (^L = formfeed), "\n" (^J = newline), "\r" (^M = return), "\t" (^I = tab), and "\v" (^K = vertical tab) accepted by printf (see "Screen Output" on page 144), as well as the notation \nnn to mean the character with octal value *nnn*.

tr is great for quick and simple translations; but for more powerful jobs consider sed, awk, or perl.

Useful options

-d   Delete the characters in *charset1* from the input.

-s   Eliminate adjacent duplicates (found in *charset1*) from the input. For example, tr -s aeiouAEIOU would squeeze adjacent, duplicate vowels to be single vowels (reeeeeeally would become really).

-c   Operate on all characters *not* found in *charset1*.

-t   If *charset1* is longer than *charset2*, make them the same length by truncating *charset1*. If -t is not present, the last character of *charset2* is (invisibly) repeated until *charset2* is the same length as *charset1*.

sort [*options*] [*files*]   coreutils

/bin		stdin	stdout	- file	-- opt	--help	--version

The sort command prints lines of text in alphabetical order, or sorted by some other rule you specify. All provided files are concatenated, and the result is sorted and printed.

```
$ cat myfile
def
```

```
xyz
abc
$ sort myfile
abc
def
xyz
```

Useful options

-f	Case-insensitive sorting.
-n	Sort numerically (i.e., 9 comes before 10) instead of alphabetically (10 comes before 9 because it begins with a "1").
-g	Another numerical sorting method with a different algorithm that, among other things, recognizes scientific notation (7.4e3 means "7.4 times ten to the third power," or 7400). Run info sort for full technical details.
-u	Unique sort: ignore duplicate lines. (If used with -c for checking sorted files, fail if any consecutive lines are identical.)
-c	Don't sort, just check if the input is already sorted. If it is, print nothing, otherwise print an error message.
-b	Ignore leading blanks.
-r	Reverse the output: sort from greatest to least.
-t X	Use X as the field delimiter for the -k option.
-k F1[.C1][,F2[.C2]]	Choose sorting keys.

A sorting key is a portion of a line that's considered when sorting, instead of considering the entire line. An example is "the fifth character of each line." Normally, sort would consider these lines to be in sorted order:

```
aaaaz
bbbby
```

but if your sorting key is "the fifth character of each line," then the lines are reversed because y comes before z. The syntax means:

Item	Meaning	Default if not supplied
F1	Starting field	Required
C1	Starting position within with field 1	1

Item	Meaning	Default if not supplied
F2	Ending field	Last field
C2	Starting position within ending field	1

So sort -k1.5 sorts based on the first field, beginning at its fifth character; and sort -k2.8,5 means "from the eighth character of the second field, to the first character of the fifth field."

You can repeat the -k option to define multiple keys, which will be applied from first to last as you specify them on the command line.

uniq [*options*] [*files*]   coreutils

/usr/bin		stdin	stdout	- file	-- opt	--help	--version

The uniq command operates on consecutive, duplicate lines of text. For example, if you have a file *myfile*:

```
$ cat myfile
a
b
b
c
b
```

then uniq would detect and process (in whatever way you specify) the two consecutive b's, but not the third b.

```
$ uniq myfile
a
b
c
b
```

uniq is often used after sorting a file:

```
$ sort myfile | uniq
a
b
c
```

In this case, only a single b remains. Also, you can count duplicate lines instead of eliminating them:

```
$ sort myfile | uniq -c
      1 a
      3 b
      1 c
```

Useful options

-c	Count adjacent duplicate lines.
-i	Case-insensitive operation.
-u	Print unique lines only.
-d	Print duplicate lines only.
-s *N*	Ignore the first *N* characters on each line when detecting duplicates.
-f *N*	Ignore the first *N* whitespace-separated fields on each line when detecting duplicates.
-w *N*	Consider only the first *N* characters on each line when detecting duplicates. If used with -s or -f, sort will ignore the specified number of characters or fields first, then consider the next *N* characters.

tee [*options*] *files*   coreutils

/usr/bin	stdin	stdout	- file	-- opt	--help	--version

Like the cat command, the tee command copies standard input to standard output unaltered. Simultaneously, however, it also copies that same standard input to one or more files. tee is most often found in the middle of pipelines, writing some intermediate data to a file while also passing it to the next command in the pipeline:

```
$ who | tee original_who | sort
```

This would print the sorted output of who on standard output, but write the original (unsorted) output of who to the file *original_who*.

Useful options

-a	Append instead of overwriting files.
-i	Ignore interrupt signals.

More Powerful Manipulations

We've just touched the tip of the iceberg for Linux text filtering. Linux has hundreds of filters that produce ever more complex manipulations of the data. But with great power comes a great learning curve, too much for a short book. Here are a few filters to get you started.

awk

awk is a pattern-matching language. It can match data by regular expression, and perform actions based on the data. Here are a few simple examples for processing a text file, *myfile*.

Print the second and fourth word on each line:

```
$ awk '{print $2, $4}' myfile
```

Print all lines that are shorter than 60 characters:

```
$ awk '{length($0) < 60}' myfile
```

sed

Like awk, sed is a pattern-matching engine that can perform manipulations on lines of text. Its syntax is closely related to that of vim and the line editor ed. Here are some trivial examples.

Print the file with all occurrences of the string "red" changed to "hat":

```
$ sed 's/red/hat/g' myfile
```

Print the file with the first 10 lines removed:

```
$ sed '1,10d' myfile
```

m4

m4 is a macro-processing language. It locates keywords within a file and substitutes values for them. For example, given this file:

```
$ cat myfile
My name is NAME and I am AGE years old
ifelse(QUOTE,yes,No matter where you go... there you are)
```

see what m4 does with substitutions for NAME, AGE, and QUOTE:

```
$ m4 -DNAME=Sandy myfile
My name is Sandy and I am AGE years old
```

```
$ m4 -DNAME=Sandy -DAGE=25 myfile
My name is Sandy and I am 25 years old

$ m4 -DNAME=Sandy -DAGE=25 -DQUOTE=yes myfile
My name is Sandy and I am 25 years old
No matter where you go... there you are
```

perl, python

Perl and Python are full-fledged scripting languages power-ful enough to build complete, robust applications.

File Compression and Packaging

gzip	Compress files with GNU Zip
gunzip	Uncompress GNU Zip files
compress	Compress files with traditional Unix compression
uncompress	Uncompress files with traditional Unix compression
zcat	Compress/uncompress file via standard input/output (gzip or compress)
bzip2	Compress files in BZip format
bunzip2	Uncompress BZip files
zip	Compress files in Windows Zip format
unzip	Uncompress Windows Zip files
uuencode	Convert file to uuencoded format
uudecode	Unconvert file from uuencoded format

Linux can compress files into a variety of formats and uncompress them. The most popular format is GNU Zip (gzip), whose compressed files are named with the *.gz* suffix. Other commonly found formats are classic Unix compres-sion (*.Z* suffix), bzip2 compression (*.bz2* suffix) and Zip files from Windows systems (*.zip* suffix).

A related technology involves converting binary files into tex-tual formats, so they can (say) be transmitted within an email message. Nowadays this is done automatically with attach-ments and MIME tools, but we'll cover the older uuencode and uudecode programs, which do still get used.

If you come across a format we don't cover, such as Macintosh hqx/sit files, Arc, Zoo, and others, you can learn more at *http://www.faqs.org/faqs/compression-faq/part1/section-2.html* and *http://www-106.ibm.com/developerworks/library/l-lw-comp.html*

gzip [*options*] [*files*]   gzip

/bin		stdin	stdout	- file	-- opt	--help	--version

gzip and gunzip compress and uncompress files in GNU Zip format. Compressed files have the suffix *.gz*.

Sample commands

gzip *file*	Compress *file* to create *file.gz*. Original *file* is deleted.
gzip -c *file*	Produce compressed data on standard output.
cat *file* | gzip	Produce compressed data from a pipeline.
gunzip *file*.gz	Uncompress *file.gz* to create *file*. Original *file.gz* is deleted.
gunzip -c *file*.gz	Uncompress the data on standard output.
cat *file*.gz | gunzip	Uncompress the data from a pipeline.
zcat *file*.z	Uncompress the data on standard output.

gzipped tar files: sample commands

tar czf *myfile*.tar.gz *dirname*	Pack directory *dirname*.
tar tzf *myfile*.tar.gz	List contents.
tar xzf *myfile*.tar.gz	Unpack.

Add the v option to tar to print filenames as they are processed.

compress [*options*] [*files*]   ncompress

/usr/bin		stdin	stdout	- file	-- opt	--help	--version

compress and uncompress compress and uncompress files in standard Unix compression format (Lempel Ziv). Compressed files have the suffix .Z.

Sample commands

`compress file`	Compress `file` to create `file.Z`. Original `file` is deleted.
`compress -c file`	Produce compressed data on standard output.
`cat file	compress`	Produce compressed data from a pipeline.
`uncompress file.Z`	Uncompress `file.Z` to create `file`. Original `file.Z` is deleted.
`uncompress -c file.Z`	Uncompress the data on standard output.
`cat file.Z	uncompress`	Uncompress the data from a pipeline.
`zcat file.Z`	Uncompress the data on standard output.

Compressed tar files: sample commands

`tar cZf myfile.tar.Z dirname`	Pack directory `dirname`.
`tar tZf myfile.tar.Z`	List contents.
`tar xZf myfile.tar.Z`	Unpack.

Add the v option to tar to print filenames as they are processed.

bzip2 [*options*] [*files*]   bzip2

/usr/bin	stdin	stdout	- file	-- opt	--help	--version

bzip2 and bunzip2 compress and uncompress files in Burrows-Wheeler format. Compressed files have the suffix *.bz2*.

Sample commands

`bzip2 file`	Compress `file` to create `file.bz2`. Original `file` is deleted.
`bzip2 -c file`	Produce compressed data on standard output.
`cat file	bzip2`	Produce compressed data on standard output.
`bunzip2 file.bz2`	Uncompress `file.bz2` to create `file`. Original `file.bz2` is deleted.
`bunzip2 -c file.bz2`	Uncompress the data on standard output.
`cat file.bz2| bunzip2`	Uncompress the data on standard output.
`bzcat file.bz2`	Uncompress the data on standard output.

bzipped tar files: sample commands

```
tar cjf myfile.tar.bz2 dirname        Pack.
tar tjf -myfile.tar.bz2               List contents.
tar xjf myfile.tar.bz2                Unpack.
```

Add the v option to tar to print filenames as they are processed.

zip [*options*] [*files*]   zip

/usr/bin		stdin	stdout	- file	-- opt	--help	--version

zip and unzip compress and uncompress files in Windows Zip
format. Compressed files have the suffix *.zip*. Unlike gzip,
compress, and bzip2, zip does not delete the original file(s).

```
zip myfile.zip file1 file2 file3...   Pack.
zip -r myfile.zip dirname             Pack recursively.
unzip -l myfile.zip                   List contents.
unzip myfile.zip                      Unpack.
```

uuencode [*options*] *newfile infile*   sharutils

/usr/bin		stdin	stdout	- file	-- opt	--help	--version

Before the days of email attachments and MIME, binary files took
some work to transmit by email. You would first uuencode the files
(pronounced "you-you-encode") into an ASCII format that looks
like this:

```
begin 644 myfile
M(R`N8V]N9FEG=7)E("UG;G4@+7=I=&@M<F5A9&QI;F4@+7=I=&@M8W5R<V5S
M=6YI9F]R;2UC;VYF:6<M<')E9FEX/2]U<W(@+75S<B]L;V-A;"LM;6%N9&ER
...
end
```

Upon receiving this data, the recipient would uudecode ("you-you-
decode") it to restore the original data.

To convert a file *myfile* into uuencoded format, creating *myfile.uu*:

```
$ uuencode newfile myfile > myfile.uu
```

The first argument, *newfile*, is the file to be created at decoding time. It will appear in the first line of uuencoded output:

```
begin 644 newfile
M(R`N N8`F7%%S:%]P<F]F:`6 @E]Q9<A^^,B, @#4(4@5=C-@$!%^7^^S=1!F%/G*>6@@]QUH2:,@!6#%)>&4G%D >>>**
...
```

To decode this uudecoded file *myfile.uu*, creating *newfile*:

```
$ uudecode myfile.uu
```

File Comparison

diff	Line-by-line comparison of two files or directories
comm	Line-by-line comparison of two sorted files
cmp	Byte-by-byte comparison of two files
md5sum	Compute a checksum of the given files (MD5)

There are three ways to compare Linux files:

- Line by line (diff, diff3, sdiff, comm), best suited to text files
- Byte by byte (cmp), often used for binary files
- By comparing checksums (md5sum, sum, cksum)

These programs are all text-based. For a graphical file-comparison tool, try xxdiff at *http://xxdiff.sourceforge.net*.

diff [*options*] *file1 file2*   diffutils

/usr/bin	stdin	stdout	- file	-- opt	--help	--version

The diff command compares two files line-by-line, or two directories. When comparing text files, diff can produce detailed reports of their differences. For binary files, diff merely reports whether they differ or not. For all files, if there are no differences, diff produces no output.

The traditional output format looks like this:

> *Indication of line numbers and the type of change*
> < *Corresponding section of file1, if any*
> ---
> > *Corresponding section of file2, if any*

For example, if we start with a file *fileA*:

```
Hello, this is a wonderful file.
The quick brown fox jumped over
the lazy dogs.
Goodbye for now.
```

Suppose we delete the first line, change "brown" to "blue" on the second line, and add a final line, creating a file *fileB*:

```
The quick blue fox jumped over
the lazy dogs.
Goodbye for now.
Linux r00lz!
```

Then diff fileA fileB produces this output:

```
1,2c1                                    fileA lines 1-2 became fileB line 1
< Hello, this is a wonderful file.       Lines 1-2 of fileA
< The quick brown fox jumped over
---                                      diff separator
> The quick blue fox jumped over         Line 1 of fileB
4a4                                      Line 4 was added
> Linux r00lz!                           The added line
```

The leading symbols < and > are arrows indicating *fileA* and *fileB*, respectively. This output format is the default: many others are available, some of which can be fed directly to other tools. Try them out to see what they look like.

Option	Output format
-n	RCS version control format, as produced by rcsdiff (man rcsdiff).
-c	Context diff format, as used by the patch command (man patch).
-D macro	C preprocessor format, using #ifdef macro ... #else ... #endif.
-u	Unified format, which merges the files and prepends "-" for deletion and "+" for addition.
-y	Side-by-side format; use -W to adjust the width of the output.
-e	Create an ed script that would change *fileA* into *fileB* if run.
-q	Don't report changes, just say whether the files differ.

diff can also compare directories:

```
$ diff dir1 dir2
```

which compares any same-named files in those directories, and lists all files that appear in one directory but not the other. If you want to compare entire directory hierarchies, recursively, use the -r option:

```
$ diff -r dir1 dir2
```

which produces a (potentially massive) report of all differences.

Useful options

-b	Don't consider whitespace.
-B	Don't consider blank lines.
-i	Ignore case.
-r	When comparing directories, recurse into subdirectories.

diff is just one member of a family of programs that operate on file differences. Some others are diff3, which compares three files at a time, and sdiff, which merges the differences between two files to create a third file according to your instructions.

comm [*options*] *file1 file2*   coreutils

/usr/bin	stdin	stdout	- file	-- opt	--help	--version

The comm command compares two sorted files and produces three columns of output, separated by tabs:

1. All lines that appear in *file1* but not in *file2*.

2. All lines that appear in *file2* but not in *file1*.

3. All lines that appear in both files.

For example, if *file1* and *file2* contain these lines:

```
file1:   file2:
apple    baker
baker    charlie
charlie  dark
```

then comm produces this output:

```
$ comm file1 file2
apple
    baker
    charlie
  dark
```

Useful options

-1	Suppress column 1.
-2	Suppress column 2.
-3	Suppress column 3.

cmp [*options*] *file1 file2* [*offset1* [*offset2*]]   diffutils

/usr/bin   stdin   stdout   - file   -- opt   --help   --version

The cmp command compares two files. If their contents are the same, cmp reports nothing, but if different, it lists the location of the first difference:

```
$ cmp myfile yourfile
myfile yourfile differ: char 494, line 17
```

By default, cmp does not tell you what the difference is, only where it is. It also is perfectly suitable for comparing binary files, as opposed to diff, which operates best on text files.

Normally, cmp starts its comparison at the beginning of each file, but it will start elsewhere if you provide offsets:

```
$ cmp myfile yourfile 10 20
```

This begins the comparison at the tenth character of *myfile* and the twentieth of *yourfile*.

Useful options

-l	Long output: print all differences, byte by byte:
	```$ cmp -l myfile yourfile```
	``` 494 164 172```
	This means at offset 494 (in decimal), *myfile* has "t" (octal 164) but *yourfile* has "z" (octal 172)

-s	Silent output: don't print anything, just exit with an appropriate return code; 0 if the files match, 1 if they don't. (Or other codes if the comparison fails for some reason.)

The md5sum command prints a 32-byte checksum of the given files, using the MD5 algorithm (see *http://www.faqs.org/rfcs/rfc1321.html* for the technical details):

```
$ md5sum myfile
dd63602df1cceb57966d085524c3980f  myfile
```

Two different files are highly unlikely to have the same MD5 checksum, so comparing checksums is a reasonably reliable way to detect if two files differ:

```
$ md5sum myfile1 > sum1
$ md5sum myfile2 > sum2
$ diff -q sum1 sum2
Files sum1 and sum2 differ
```

or if a set of files has changed, using --check:

```
$ md5sum file1 file2 file3 > mysum
$ md5sum --check mysum
file1: OK
file2: OK
file3: OK
$ echo "new data" > file2
$ md5sum --check mysum
file1: OK
file2: FAILED
file3: OK
md5sum: WARNING: 1 of 3 computed checksums did NOT match
```

Two other programs similar to md5sum are sum and cksum, which use different algorithms to compute their checksums. sum is compatible with other Unix systems, specifically BSD Unix (the default) or System V Unix (-s option), and cksum produces a CRC checksum:

```
$ sum myfile
12410     3
$ sum -s myfile
47909 6 myfile
$ cksum myfile
1204834076 2863 myfile
```

The first integer is a checksum and the second is a block count. But as you can see, these checksums are small numbers and therefore unreliable, since files could have identical checksums by coincidence. md5sum is by far the best.

Disks and Filesystems

df	Display available space on mounted filesystems
mount	Make a disk partition accessible
umount	Unmount a disk partition (make it inaccessible)
fsck	Check a disk partition for errors
sync	Flush all disk caches to disk

Linux systems can have multiple disks or disk partitions. In casual conversation, these are variously called disks, partitions, filesystems, volumes, even directories. We'll try to be more accurate.

A *disk* is a hardware device, which may be divided into *partitions* that act as independent storage devices. Partitions are represented on Linux systems as special files in (usually) the */dev* directory. For example, */dev/hda7* could be a partition on your master IDE disk. Some common devices in */dev* are:

hda	First IDE bus, master device; partitions are *hda1*, *hda2*, ...
hdb	First IDE bus, slave device; partitions are *hdb1*, *hdb2*, ...
hdc	Second IDE bus, master device; partitions are *hdc1*, *hdc2*, ...
hdd	Second IDE bus, slave device; partitions are *hdd1*, *hdd2*, ...
sda	First SCSI device; partitions are *sda1*, *sda2*, ...
sdb	Second SCSI device; partitions are *sdb1*, *sdb2*, ... Likewise for *sdc*, *sdd*, ...
ht0	First IDE tape drive (then *ht1*, *ht2*, ...) with auto-rewind
nht0	First IDE tape drive (then *nht1*, *nht2*, ...) without auto-rewind
st0	First SCSI tape drive (then *st1*, *st2*, ...)
scd0	First SCSI CD-ROM drive (then *scd1*, *scd2*, ...)
fd0	First floppy drive (then *fd1*, *fd2*, ...), usually mounted on */mnt/floppy*

Before a partition can hold files, it is "formatted" by writing a *filesystem* on it. A filesystem defines how files are represented; examples are ext3 (Linux journaling filesystem, the Fedora default) and vfat (Microsoft Windows filesystem). Formatting is generally done for you when installing Linux.

Once a filesystem is created, you can make it available for use by *mounting* it on an empty directory. For example, if you mount a Windows filesystem on a directory */mnt/win*, it becomes part of your system's directory tree, and you can create and edit files like */mnt/win/myfile*. Filesystems can also be unmounted to make them inaccessible, say, for maintenance. Mounting of hard drives is generally done automatically at boot time.

df [*options*] [*disk devices*| *files*| *directories*]   coreutils

/bin		stdin	stdout	- file	-- opt	--help	--version

The df (disk free) program shows you the size, used space, and free space on a given disk partition. If you supply a file or directory, df describes the disk device on which that file or directory resides. With no arguments, df reports on all mounted filesystems.

```
$ df
Filesystem       1k-blocks     Used Available Use% Mounted on
/dev/hda          1011928    225464    735060  24% /
/dev/hda9          521748    249148    246096  51% /var
/dev/hda8         8064272   4088636   3565984  54% /usr
/dev/hda10        8064272   4586576   3068044  60% /home
```

Useful options

-k -m	List all sizes in kilobytes (the default) or megabytes, respectively.
-B *N*	Display sizes in blocks that you define, where 1 block = *N* bytes. (Default = 1024).
-h -H	Print "human readable" output, and choose the most appropriate unit for each size. For example, if your two disks have 1 gigabyte and 25 kilobytes free, respectively, df -h prints 1G and 25K. The -h option uses powers of 1024, whereas -H uses powers of 1000.
-l	Display only local filesystems, not networked filesystems.
-T	Include the filesystem type (ext2, vfat, etc.) in the output.
-t *type*	Display only filesystems of the given type.
-x *type*	Don't display filesystems of the given type.
-i	Inode mode. Display total, used, and free inodes for each filesystem, instead of disk blocks.

mount [*options*] *device* | *directory*   mount

/bin   stdin   stdout   - file   -- opt   --help   --version

The mount command makes a hardware storage device accessible.
Most commonly it handles disk devices (say, */dev/hda1*), making
them accessible via an existing directory (say, */mnt/mydir*):

```
# mkdir /mnt/mydir
# mount /dev/hda1 /mnt/mydir
# df /mnt/mydir
Filesystem      1K-blocks    Used Available Use% Mounted on
/dev/hda1        1011928  285744    674780  30% /mnt/mydir
```

mount has tons of options and uses; we will discuss only the most
basic.

In most common cases, mount reads the file */etc/fstab* (filesystem
table) to learn how to mount a desired disk. For example, if you
type mount */usr*, the mount command looks up the "/usr" line in
/etc/fstab, which might look like this:

```
/dev/hda8    /usr    ext3    defaults    1    2
```

Here mount learns, among other things, that disk device */dev/hda8*
should be mounted on */usr* as a Linux ext3-formatted filesystem.[*]

mount is run typically by the superuser, but common devices like
floppy and CD-ROM drives often can be mounted and
unmounted by any user.

```
$ mount /mnt/cdrom
$ mount /mnt/floppy
```

umount [*options*] [*device* | *directory*]   mount

/bin   stdin   stdout   - file   -- opt   --help   --version

umount is the opposite of mount: it makes a disk partition unavail-
able. For instance, if you've mounted a CD-ROM disc, you can't
eject it until it's unmounted:

```
$ umount /mnt/cdrom
```

Always unmount removable media before ejecting it or you risk
damage to its filesystem. To unmount all mounted devices:

```
# umount -a
```

---

[*] Alternatively, you can use the -t option of mount to specify the filesystem
type directly, such as mount -t ext3 /dev/hda1 /mnt/mydir. See man mount.

Don't unmount a filesystem that's in use; in fact, the umount command will refuse to do so for safety reasons.

fsck [options] [devices]

e2fsprogs

/sbin   stdin   **stdout**   - file   -- opt   --help   --version

The fsck (filesystem check) command validates a Linux disk partition and, if requested, repairs errors found on it. fsck is run
automatically when your system boots; however, you can run it
manually if you like. In general, unmount a device before checking
it, so no other programs are operating on it at the same time:

```
# umount /dev/hda10
# fsck -f /dev/hda10
Pass 1: Checking inodes, blocks, and sizes
Pass 2: Checking directory structure
Pass 3: Checking directory connectivity
Pass 4: Checking reference counts
Pass 5: Checking group summary information
/home: 172/1281696 files (11.6% non-contiguous), 1405555/
2562359 blocks
```

fsck is a frontend for a set of filesystem-checking programs found
in */sbin*, with names beginning "fsck". Only certain types of filesystems are supported; you can list them with the command:

```
$ ls /sbin/fsck.* | cut -d. -f2
```

Useful options

-A   Check all disks listed in */etc/fstab*, in order.

-N   Print a description of the checking that would be done, but exit without
performing any checking.

-r   Fix errors interactively, prompting before each fix.

-a   Fix errors automatically (only if you *really* know what you're doing; if not,
you can seriously mess up a filesystem).

sync

coreutils

/bin   stdin   stdout   - file   -- opt   **--help**   --version

The sync command flushes all disk caches to disk. Usually, the
kernel may buffer reads, writes, inode changes, and other disk-
related activity in memory. sync writes the changes to disk.

Normally, you don't need to run this command, but if (say) you're about to do something risky that might crash your machine, running sync immediately beforehand can't hurt.

Partitioning and Formatting Disks

Disk-related operations like partitioning and formatting can be complex on Linux systems. Here are pointers to the programs you may need (start with their manpages).

parted, fdisk, or sfdisk	Partition a hard drive. Any of these programs will do: they simply have different user interfaces.
mkfs	Format a hard disk, i.e., create a new filesystem.
floppy	Format a floppy disk.

Backups and Remote Storage

mt	Control a tape drive
dump	Write a disk partition to tape
restore	Restore the results of a dump
tar	Read and write tape archives
cdrecord	Burn a CD-R
rsync	Mirror a set of files onto another device or host

There are various way to back up your precious Linux files:

- Copy them to a tape drive
- Burn them onto a CD-R
- Mirror them to a remote machine

Your tape backup device is usually */dev/ht0* for an IDE drive, or */dev/st0* for a SCSI drive (or for an IDE drive using ide-scsi emulation). It's common to make a link called */dev/tape* to the appropriate device:

```
$ ln -s /dev/ht0 /dev/tape
```

We aren't presenting every Linux command for backups. Some users prefer cpio to tar, and for low-level disk copies, dd is invaluable. See the manpages for these programs if you are interested in them.

mt [-f *device*] *command*

/bin		stdin	stdout	- file	-- opt	--help	--version

The mt (magnetic tape) command performs simple operations on a tape drive, such as rewinding, skipping forward and backward, and retensioning. Some common operations are:

status	Show the status of the drive.
rewind	Rewind the tape.
retension	Retension the tape.
erase	Erase the tape.
offline	Take the tape drive offline.
eod	Move forward on the tape to the end of data.

For example:

```
$ mt -f /dev/tape rewind
```

You can also move through the tape, file by file or record by record, but often you'll use a tape reading/writing program for that, such as tar or restore.

dump [*options*] *partition_or_files*

/sbin		stdin	stdout	- file	-- opt	--help	--version

The dump command writes an entire disk partition, or selected files, to a backup medium such as tape. It supports full and incremental backups, automatically figuring out which files need to be backed up (i.e., which have changed since the last backup). To restore files from the backup medium, use the restore command.

To perform a full backup of a given filesystem (say, */usr*) to your tape device (say, */dev/tape*), use the -0 (zero) and -u options:

```
# dump -0 -u -f /dev/tape /usr
```

This is called a *level zero* dump. The -u option writes a note to the file */etc/dumpdates* to say that the backup was performed.

Incremental backups may have levels 1 through 9: a level i backup stores all new and changed files since the last level $i-1$ backup.

```
# dump -1 -u -f /dev/tape /usr
```

Don't run dump on a "live" filesystem actively in use: unmount it first when possible.

restore [*options*] [*files*] dump

/sbin   stdin   **stdout**   - file   -- opt   --help   --version

The restore command reads a backup created by dump. It can then restore the files to disk, compare them against those on disk, and other operations. The friendliest way to use restore is with the -i flag for interactive operation, which lets you browse the tape contents just like a filesystem, selecting files and directories, and finally restoring them.

```
# restore -i -f /dev/tape
```

restore then prompts you for commands like the ones listed below.

help	Print a help message.
quit	Exit the program without restoring any files.
cd *directory*	Like the shell's cd command, set your current working directory within the dump for working with files.
ls	Like the Linux ls command, view all files in the current working directory within the dump.
pwd	Like the shell's pwd command, print the name of your current working directory within the dump.
add	Add files or directories to the "extraction list:" the list of files you'll want to restore. With no arguments, add adds the current directory and all its files.
add *filename*	Add the file *filename* to the extraction list.
add *dir*	Add the directory *dir* to the extraction list.
delete	The opposite of add: remove files from the extraction list. If run with no arguments, delete removes the current directory (and its contents) from the extraction list.
delete *filename*	Remove the file *myfile* from the extraction list.
delete *dir*	Remove the directory *dir* from the extraction list.
extract	Restore all the files you added to the extraction list. (Tip: if your backup spans multiple tapes, start with the last tape and work backwards.)

restore also works in other noninteractive modes:

restore -x	Restore everything from the tape into an existing filesystem. (cd into the root of the desired filesystem first.)
restore -r	Restore everything from the tape into a freshly formatted disk partition. (cd into the root of the desired filesystem first.)
restore -t	List the contents of the dump.
restore -C	Compare the dump against the original filesystem.

tar [*options*] [*files*]   tar

/bin	stdin	stdout	- file	-- opt	--help	--version

The tar (tape archive) program does more than read and write files to and from a tape drive:

```
$ tar -cf /dev/tape myfile1 myfile2
```

it also lets you create and extract from *tar files*, which are a standard means of packaging files on Linux and Unix systems:

```
$ tar -czvf myarchive.tar.gz mydir      Create
$ tar -tzvf myarchive.tar.gz            List contents
$ tar -xzvf myarchive.tar.gz            Extract
```

If you specify files on the command line, only those files are processed:

```
$ tar -xvf /dev/tape file1 file2 file3
```

Otherwise the entire archive is processed.

Useful options

-c	Create an archive. You'll have to list the input files and directories on the command line.
-r	Append files to an existing archive.
-u	Append new/changed files to an existing archive.
-A	Append one archive (e.g., a *tar* file) to the end of another archive: e.g., tar -A -f /dev/tape myfile.tar.
-t	List the archive.
-x	Extract files from the archive.

`-f` *file*	Read the archive from, or write the archive to, the given file. This could be a device (such as */dev/tape*) or a plain file if you want to create a traditional Linux *tar* file.
`-d`	Diff (compare) the archive against the filesystem.
`-z`	Compress (while writing) or uncompress (while reading) the data with `gzip`.
`-j`	Compress (while writing) or uncompress (while reading) the data with `bzip2`.
`-Z`	Compress (while writing) or uncompress (while reading) the data with Unix `compress`.
`-b` *N*	Use a block size of *N* * 512 bytes.
`-v`	Verbose mode: print extra information.
`-h`	Follow symbolic links.
`-l`	Do not cross filesystem boundaries.
`-p`	When extracting files, restore their original permissions and ownership.

cdrecord [*options*] *tracks* cdrecord

/usr/bin		stdin	stdout	- file	-- opt	--help	--version

The cdrecord command burns a CD-R disc on a SCSI CD writer, or an IDE CD writer using Linux ide-scsi emulation. To burn the contents of a directory onto a CD-ROM readable on Linux, Windows, and Macintosh systems:[*]

1. Locate your CD writer's device by running:

```
$ cdrecord --scanbus
...
0,0,0    0) *
0,1,0    1) *
0,2,0    2) *
0,3,0    3) 'YAMAHA  ' 'CRW6416S ' '1.0d' Removable
CD-ROM
...
```

The device in this case is 0,3,0.

2. Find out your CD writer's speed for writing CD-R or CD-RW discs (whichever you're using). Suppose it is a 6x writer of CD-Rs, so the speed is 6.

---

[*] Specifically, an ISO9660 CD with Rock Ridge extensions. mkisofs can create other formats for cdrecord to burn: see man mkisofs.

3. Put the files you want to burn into a directory, say, *dir*. Arrange them exactly as you'd like them on the CD. The directory *dir* itself will not be copied to CD, just its contents.

4. Burn the CD:

```
$ DEVICE="0,3,0"
$ SPEED=6
$ mkisofs -R -l dir > mydisk.iso
$ cdrecord -v dev=${DEVICE} speed=${SPEED} mydisk.iso
```

or if your system is fast enough, you can do this with a single pipeline:

```
$ mkisofs -R -l dir \
  | cdrecord -v dev=${DEVICE} speed=${SPEED} -
```

cdrecord can burn music CDs as well, but you might want to use a friendlier, graphical program like xcdroast instead (see "Audio and Video" on page 163), which is built on top of cdrecord.

rsync [*options*] *source destination*   rsync

/usr/bin		stdin	stdout	- file	-- opt	--help	--version

The rsync command copies a set of files. It can make an exact copy, including file permissions and other attributes (called *mirroring*), or it can just copy the data. It can run over a network or on a single machine. rsync has many uses and over 50 options; we'll present just a few common cases relating to backups.

To mirror the directory *D1* and its contents into another directory *D2* on a single machine:

```
$ rsync -a D1 D2
```

In order to mirror directory *D1* over the network to another host, *server.example.com*, where you have an account with username smith, securing the connection with SSH to prevent eavesdropping:

```
$ rsync -a -e ssh D1 smith@server.example.com:
```

Useful options

-o	Copy the ownership of the files. (You probably need superuser privileges on the remote host.)
-g	Copy the group ownership of the files. (You might need superuser privileges on the remote host.)

-p	Copy the file permissions.
-t	Copy the file timestamps.
-r	Copy directories recursively, i.e., including their contents.
-l	Permit symbolic links to be copied (not the files they point to).
-D	Permit devices to be copied. (Superuser only.)
-a	Mirroring: copy all attributes of the original files. This implies all of the options, -Dgloprt.
-v	Verbose mode: print information about what's happening during the copy. Add --progress to display a numeric progress meter while files are copied.
-e *command*	Specify a different remote shell program such as ssh for more security.

File Printing

lpr	Print a file
lpq	View the print queue
lprm	Remove a print job from the queue

Linux has two popular printing systems, called CUPS and LPRng; Fedora comes with CUPS. Both systems use commands with the same names: lpr, lpq, and lprm. However, these commands have different options depending whether you're using CUPS or LPRng. To be generally helpful, we will present common options that work with both systems.

To install a printer for use with Fedora, run the command:

```
# redhat-config-printer
```

and follow the directions.

lpr [*options*] [*files*]   cups

/usr/bin	stdin	stdout	- file	-- opt	--help	--version

The lpr (line printer) command sends a file to a printer.

```
$ lpr -P myprinter myfile
```

Useful options

-P *printername*	Send the file to printer *printername*, which you have previously set up with redhat-config-printer.
-# *N*	Print *N* copies of the file.
-J *name*	Set the job *name* that prints on the cover page (if your system is set up to print cover pages).

lpq [*options*]   cups

/usr/bin	stdin	**stdout**	- file	-- opt	--help	--version

The lpq (line printer queue) command lists all print jobs waiting to be printed.

Useful options

-P *printername*	List the queue for printer *printername*.
-a	List the queue for all printers.
-l	Be verbose: display information in a longer format.

lprm [*options*] [*job_IDs*]   cups

/usr/bin	stdin	**stdout**	- file	-- opt	--help	--version

The lprm (line printer remove) command cancels one or more print jobs. Use lpq to learn the ID of the desired print jobs (say, 61 and 78), then type:

```
$ lprm -P printername 61 78
```

If you don't supply any job IDs, your current print job is canceled. (Only the superuser can cancel other users' jobs.) The -P option specifies which print queue contains the job.

Spelling Operations

look	Look up the spelling of a word quickly
aspell	Interactive spelling checker
spell	Batch spelling checker

Linux has several spellcheckers built in. If you're accustomed to graphical spellcheckers, you might find Linux's fairly primitive, but they can be used in pipelines, which is quite powerful.

look [*options*] *prefix* [*dictionary_file*]   util-linux

/usr/bin		stdin	**stdout**	- file	-- opt	--help	--version

The look command prints (on standard output) words that begin with a given string *prefix*. The words are located in a dictionary file (default */usr/share/dict/words)*. For instance, look bigg prints:

```
bigger
biggest
Biggs
```

If you supply your own dictionary file—any text file with alphabetically sorted lines—look will print all lines beginning with the given *prefix*.

Useful options

-f   Ignore case.

-t *X*   Match the prefix only up to and including the termination character *X*. For instance, look -t i big prints all words beginning with "bi".

aspell [*options*] *file* | *command*   aspell

/usr/bin		stdin	stdout	- file	-- opt	--help	--version

aspell is a powerful spellchecker with dozens of options. A few useful commands are:

aspell -c *file*
> Interactively check, and optionally correct, the spelling of all words in file.

aspell -l < *file*
> Print a list of the misspelled words in *file* on standard output.

aspell dump master
> Print aspell's master dictionary on standard output.

aspell help
> Print a concise help message. See *http://aspell.net* for more information.

spell [*files*]   aspell

/usr/bin	stdin	stdout	- file	-- opt	--help	--version

The spell command prints all words in the given files that are
misspelled, according to its dictionary. It's the same as:

```
$ cat files | aspell -l | sort -u
```

If no files are supplied, spell reads from standard input.

Viewing Processes

ps	List process
uptime	View the system load
w	List active processes for all users
top	Monitor resource-intensive processes interactively
xload	Monitor system load graphically in an X window
free	Display free memory

A *process* is a unit of work on a Linux system. Each program
you run represents one or more processes, and Linux provides commands for viewing and manipulating them. Every
process is identified by a numeric *process ID*, or PID.

Processes are not the same as jobs (see "Job Control" on
page 29): processes are part of the operating system, whereas
jobs are known only to the shell in which they're running. A
running program comprises one or more processes; a job consists of one or more programs executed as a shell command.

ps [*options*]   procps

/bin	stdin	stdout	- file	-- opt	--help	--version

The ps command displays information about your running
processes, and optionally the processes of other users.

```
$ ps
  PID TTY          TIME CMD
 4706 pts/2    00:00:01 bash
15007 pts/2    00:00:00 emacs
16729 pts/2    00:00:00 ps
```

ps has at least 80 options; we'll cover just a few useful combinations. If the options seem arbitrary or inconsistent, it's because the supplied ps command (GNU ps) incorporates the features of several other Unix ps commands, attempting to be compatible with all of them.

To view your processes:

```
$ ps -ux
```

all of user smith's processes:

```
$ ps -U smith
```

all occurrences of a program:

```
$ ps -C program_name
```

processes on terminal N:

```
$ ps -tN
```

particular processes 1, 2, and 3505:

```
$ ps -p1,2,3505
```

all processes with command lines truncated to screen width:

```
$ ps -ef
```

all processes with full command lines:

```
$ ps -efww
```

and all processes in a threaded view, which indents child processes below their parents:

```
$ ps -efH
```

Remember, you can extract information more finely from the output of ps using grep or other filter programs.

uptime procps

/usr/bin		stdin	stdout	-file	--opt	--help	--version

The uptime command tells you how long the system has been running since the last boot.

```
$ uptime
 10:54pm  up 8 days,  3:44,  3 users,  load average: 0.89,
 1.00, 2.15
```

This information is, from right to left: the current time (10:54pm), system uptime (8 days, 3 hours, 44 minutes), number of users logged in (3), and system load average for three time periods: one minute (0.89), five minutes (1.00), and fifteen minutes (2.15). The load average is the average number of processes ready to run in that time interval.

w [*username*]

procps

/usr/bin   stdin **stdout** - file -- opt --help --version

The w command displays the current process for each logged-in user, or more specifically, for each shell of each user:

```
$ w
 10:51pm  up 8 days,  3:42,  8 users,
 load average: 0.00, 0.00, 0.00
 USER    TTY  FROM  LOGIN@   IDLE  JCPU  PCPU WHAT
 barrett pts/0 :0    Sat 2pm 27:13m 0.07s 0.07s emacs
 jones   pts/1 host1 6Sep03  2:33m 0.74s 0.21s bash
 smith   pts/2 host2 6Sep03  0.00s 13.35s 0.04s w
```

The top line is the same one printed by uptime. The columns indicate the user's terminal, originating host or X display (if applicable), login time, idle time, two measures of the CPU time (run man w for details), and the current process. Provide a username to see only that user's information.

For the briefest output, try w -hfs.

Useful options

-h   Don't print the header line.

-f   Don't print the FROM column.

-s   Don't print the JCPU and PCPU columns.

top [*options*]

procps

/usr/bin   stdin **stdout** - file -- opt --help --version

The top command lets you monitor the most active processes, updating the display at regular intervals (say, every second). It is a screen-based program that updates the display in place, interactively.

```
$ top
116 processes: 104 sleeping, 1 running, 0 zombie, 11 stopped
CPU states: 1.1% user, 0.5% system, 0.0% nice, 4.5% idle
```

```
Mem: 523812K av, 502328K used, 21484K free, 0K shrd, 160436K
buff
Swap:  530104K av,  0K used, 530104K free  115300K cached

PID   USER PRI NI SIZE RSS SHARE STAT %CPU %MEM  TIME COMMAND
26265 smith 10 0  1092 1092 840   R    4.7  0.2  0:00 top
    1 root   0 0   540  540 472   S    0.0  0.1  0:07 init
    2 root   0 0     0    0   0   SW    0.0  0.0  0:00 kflushd
...
```

While top is running, you can press keys to change its behavior,
such as setting the update speed (s), hiding idle processes (i), or
killing processes (k). Type h to see a complete list and q to quit.

Useful options

-n*N*	Perform *N* updates, then quit.
-d*N*	Update the display every *N* seconds.
-p*N* -p*M* ...	Display only the processes with PID *N, M,* ..., up to 20 processes.
-c	Display the command-line arguments of processes.
-b	Print on standard output noninteractively, without playing screen tricks. top -b -n1 > outfile saves a quick snapshot to a file.

xload   XFree86-tools

/usr/X11R6/bin   stdin   stdout   - file   -- opt   --help   --version

Run xload to see a graphical display of the system load in an X
window. It graphs processor load (Y axis) over time (X axis).

Useful options

-update *N*	Update the display every *N* seconds (default 10).
-scale *N*	Divide the Y axis into *N* sections (default 1). xload may add more divisions as the load goes up; *N* is the minimum visible at any time.
-hl *color*	Use this *color* for the scale divider lines.
-label *X*	Print the text *X* above the graph (default = your hostname).
-nolabel	Don't print any text label above the graph.
-jumpscroll *N*	When the graph reaches the right margin, scroll *N* pixels to the left and keep drawing (default is half the window width).

free [*options*]   procps

/usr/bin   stdin   **stdout**   - file   -- opt   **--help**   **--version**

The free command displays memory usage in kilobytes:

```
$ free
              total      used      free    shared
buffers      cached
Mem:         523812    491944     31868         0
67856       199276
-/+ buffers/cache:     224812    299000
Swap:        530104         0    530104
```

The Linux kernel reserves as much memory as possible for caching purposes, so your best estimate of free RAM in the preceding output is 299000.

Useful options

-s *N*	Run continuously and update the display every *N* seconds.
-b	Display amounts in bytes or megabytes, respectively.
-m	
-t	Add a totals line at the bottom.
-o	Don't display the "buffers/cache" line.

Controlling Processes

kill	Terminate a process (or send it a signal)
nice	Invoke a program at a particular priority
renice	Change a process's priority as it runs

Once processes are started, they can be stopped, restarted, killed, and reprioritized. We discussed some of these operations as handled by the shell in "Job Control" on page 29. Now we cover killing and reprioritizing.

kill [*options*] [*process_ids*]   **bash**

shell built-in   stdin **stdout** - file -- opt --help --version

The kill command sends a signal to a process. This can terminate a process (the default), interrupt it, suspend it, crash it, and
so on. You must own the process, or be the superuser, to affect it.

    $ kill 13243

If this does not work—some programs catch this signal without
terminating—add the -KILL option:

    $ kill -KILL 13243

which is virtually guaranteed to work. However, this is not a clean
exit for the program, which may leave resources allocated (or
other inconsistencies) upon its death.

If you don't know the PID of a process, try the pidof command:

    $ /sbin/pidof emacs

or run ps and examine the output.

In addition to the program */bin/kill* in the filesystem, most shells
have built-in kill commands, but their syntax and behavior differ.
However, they all support this usage:

    $ kill -*N* *PID*
    $ kill -*NAME* *PID*

where *N* is a signal number, and *NAME* is a signal name without its
leading "SIG" (e.g., use -HUP to send the SIGHUP signal). To see a
complete list of signals transmitted by kill, run kill -1, though
its output differs depending which kill you're running. For
descriptions of the signals, run man 7 signal.

nice [- *priority*] *command_line*   **coreutils**

/bin   stdin **stdout** - file -- opt **--help** --version

When invoking a system-intensive program, you might want to be
nice to the other processes (and users) by lowering its priority.
That's what the nice command is for. Here's an example of
setting a big job to run at priority 7:

    $ nice -7 sort VeryLargeFile > outfile

If you don't specify a priority, 10 is used. To find out the default priority (i.e., what you'd get if you didn't run nice), type nice with no arguments:

```
$ nice
0
```

If you're the superuser, you can also raise the priority (lower the number):

```
$ nice --10
```

(Yes, that's "dash negative 10".) To see the nice levels of your jobs, use ps and look at the "NI" column:

```
$ ps -o pid,user,args,nice
```

renice *priority* [*options*] *PID*   util-linux

/usr/bin		stdin	**stdout**	- file	**-- opt**	--help	--version

While the nice command can invoke a program at a given priority, renice changes the priority of an already-running process. Here we increase the nice level (decrease the priority) of process 28734 by five:

```
$ renice +5 -p 28734
```

Ordinary users can decrease priorities (increase the number), and the superuser can increase priorities (decrease the number). The valid range is −20 to +20, but avoid highly negative numbers or you might interfere with vital system processes.

Useful options

-p *pid*   Affect the given process ID. You can omit the -p and just provide a PID (renice +5 28734).

-u *username*   Affect all processes owned by the given user.

Users and Their Environment

logname	Print your login name
whoami	Print your current, effective username
id	Print the user ID and group membership of a user

who	List logged-in users, long output
users	List logged-in users, short output
finger	Print information about users
last	Determine when someone last logged in
printenv	Print your environment

Who are you? Only the system knows for sure. This grab-bag of programs tells you all about *users*: their names, login times, and properties of their environment.

logname   coreutils

| */usr/bin* | | stdin | **stdout** | - file | -- opt | **--help** | **--version** |

The logname command prints your login name. It might seem trivial, but it's useful in shell scripts.

```
$ logname
smith
```

whoami   coreutils

| */usr/bin* | | stdin | **stdout** | - file | -- opt | **--help** | **--version** |

The whoami command prints the name of the current, effective user. This may differ from your login name (the output of logname) if you've used the su command. This example distinguishes whoami from logname:

```
$ logname
smith
$ whoami
smith

$ su
Password: ********
# logname
smith
# whoami
root
```

id [*options*] [*username*]

coreutils

/usr/bin   stdin   **stdout**   - file   -- opt   --help   --version

Every user has a unique, numeric *user ID*, and a default group with a unique, numeric *group ID*. The id command prints these values along with their associated user and group names:

```
$ id
uid=500(smith) gid=500(smith)
groups=500(smith),6(disk),490(src),501(cdwrite)
```

Useful options

-u   Print the effective user ID and exit.

-g   Print the effective group ID and exit.

-G   Print the IDs of all other groups to which the user belongs.

-n   Print names (for users and groups) rather than numeric IDs. Must be
          combined with -u, -g, or -G. For example, id -Gn produces the same
          output as the groups command.

-r   Print real values instead of effective values. Must be combined with -u, -g,
          or -G.

who [*options*] [*filename*]

coreutils

/usr/bin   stdin   **stdout**   - file   -- opt   --help   --version

The who command lists all logged-in users, one user shell per line:

```
$ who
smith     :0       Sep  6 17:09
barrett   pts/1    Sep  6 17:10
jones     pts/2    Sep  8 20:58
jones     pts/4    Sep  3 05:11
```

Normally, who gets its data from the file */var/run/utmp*. The *filename* argument can specify a different data file, such as */var/log/wtmp* for past logins or */var/log/btmp* for failed logins.[*]

Useful options

-H   Print a row of headings as the first line.

-l   For remotely logged-in users, print the hostnames of origin.

---

[*] If your system is configured to log those past or failed logins.

-u	Also print each user's idle time at his/her terminal.
-T	Also indicate whether each user's terminal is writable (see mesg y in "Instant Messaging" on page 142). A plus sign means yes, a minus sign means no, and a question mark means unknown.
-m	Display information only about yourself, i.e., the user associated with the current terminal.
-q	Quick display of usernames only, and a count of users. Much like the users command, but it adds a count.

users [*filename*]   coreutils

/usr/bin		stdin	stdout	- file	-- opt	--help	--version

The users command prints a quick listing of users who have login
sessions. If a user is running multiple shells, she appears multiple
times.

```
$ users
barrett jones smith smith smith
```

Like the who command, users reads */var/log/utmp* by default but
can read from another supplied file instead.

finger [*options*] [*user*[*@host*]]   finger

/usr/bin		stdin	stdout	- file	-- opt	--help	--version

The finger command prints user information in a short form:

```
$ finger
Login    Name            Tty      Idle  Login Time
smith    Sandy Smith     :0             Sep  6 17:09
barrett  Daniel Barrett  :pts/1     24  Sep  6 17:10
jones    Jill Jones      :pts/2         Sep  8 20:58
```

or a long form:

```
$ finger smith
Login: smith              Name: Sandy Smith
Directory: /home/smith            Shell: /bin/bash
On since Sat Sep  6 17:09 (EDT) on :0
Last login Mon Sep  8 21:07 (EDT) on pts/6 from localhost
No mail.
Project:
Enhance world peace
Plan:
Mistrust first impulses; they are always right.
```

The *user* argument can be a local username or a remote user in the form *user@host*. Remote hosts will respond to finger requests only if they are configured to do so.

Useful options

-l	Print in long format.
-s	Print in short format.
-p	Don't display the Project and Plan sections, which are ordinarily read from the user's ~/.project and ~/.plan files, respectively.

last [*options*] [*users*] [*ttys*]   SysVinit

/usr/bin		stdin	**stdout**	- file	-- **opt**	--help	--version

The last command displays a history of logins, in reverse chronological order.

```
$ last
barrett  pts/3  localhost  Mon Sep 8 21:07 - 21:08  (00:01)
smith    pts/6  :0         Mon Sep 8 20:25 - 20:56  (00:31)
barrett  pts/4  myhost     Sun Sep 7 22:19 still logged in
...
```

You may provide usernames or tty names to limit the output.

Useful options

-N	Print only the latest *N* lines of output, where *N* is a positive integer.
-i	Display IP addresses instead of hostnames.
-R	Don't display hostnames.
-x	Also display system shutdowns and changes in system runlevel (e.g., from single-user mode into multiuser mode).
-f *filename*	Read from some other data file than /var/run/utmp; see the who command for more details.

printenv [*environment_variables*]   coreutils

/usr/bin		stdin	stdout	- file	-- opt	--help	--version

The printenv command prints all environment variables known to your shell and their values:

```
$ printenv
HOME=/home/smith
MAIL=/var/spool/mail/smith
```

```
NAME=Sandy Smith
SHELL=/bin/bash
...
```

or only specified variables:

```
$ printenv HOME SHELL
/home/smith
/bin/bash
```

Working with User Accounts

useradd	Create a new account
userdel	Delete an account
usermod	Modify an account
passwd	Change a password
chfn	Change a user's personal information
chsh	Change a user's shell

The Fedora installer prompts you to create two accounts, one for the superuser and one for an ordinary user (presumably yourself). But you might want to create other accounts, too.

Creating users is an important job not to be taken lightly. Every account is a potential avenue for an intruder to enter your system, so every user should have a strong, hard-to-guess password, and should change it regularly.

useradd [*options*] *username*   shadow-utils

/usr/sbin	stdin	**stdout**	- file	-- **opt**	--help	--version

The useradd command lets the superuser create a new user account.

```
# useradd smith
```

Its defaults are not very useful (run useradd -D to see them), so be sure to supply all desired options. For example:

```
# useradd -d /home/smith -s /bin/bash -g users smith
```

Useful options

-d *dir*	Set the user's home directory to be *dir*.
-s *shell*	Set the user's login shell to be *shell*.
-u *uid*	Set the user's ID to be *uid*. Unless you know what you're doing, omit this option and accept the default.
-g *group*	Set the user's initial (default) group to *group*, which can either be a numeric group ID or a group name, and which must already exist.
-G *group1,group2,...*	Make the user a member of the additional, existing groups *group1, group2*, and so on.
-m	Copy all files from your system skeleton directory, */etc/skel*, into the newly created home directory. The skeleton directory traditionally contains minimal (skeletal) versions of initialization files, like *~/.bash_profile*, to get new users started If you prefer to copy from a different directory, add the -k option (-k *your_preferred_directory*).

userdel [-r] *username*   shadow-utils

/usr/sbin	stdin	**stdout**	- file	-- opt	--help	--version

The userdel command deletes an existing user.

```
# userdel smith
```

It does not delete the files in the user's home directory unless you supply the -r option. Think carefully before deleting a user; consider deactivating the account instead (with usermod -L). And make sure you have backups of all the user's files before deleting them: you might need them again someday.

usermod [*options*] *username*   shadow-utils

/usr/sbin	stdin	**stdout**	- file	-- opt	--help	--version

The usermod command modifies the given user's account in various ways, like changing a home directory:

```
# usermod -d /home/another smith
```

Useful options

-d *dir*	Change the user's home directory to *dir*.
-l *username*	Change the user's login name to *username*. Think carefully before doing this, in case anything on your system depends on the original name. And definitely don't do it to system accounts (root, daemon, and so on)!

`-s shell`	Change the user's login shell to *shell*.
`-g group`	Change the user's initial (default) group to *group*, which can either be a numeric group ID or a group name, and which must already exist.
`-G group1,group2,...`	Make the user a member *only* of the additional, existing groups *group1*, *group2*, and so on. If the user previously belonged to other groups, but you don't specify them here, the user will no longer belong to them.
`-L`	Disable the account so the user cannot log in.
`-U`	Unlock the account after a `-L` operation.

passwd [*options*] [*username*]   passwd

/usr/bin	stdin	stdout	- file	-- opt	--help	--version

The passwd command changes a login password, yours by default:

```
# passwd
```

or another user's password if run by the superuser:

```
# passwd smith
```

passwd does have options, most of them related to password expiration. Use them only in the context of a well-thought-out security policy.

chfn [*options*] [*username*]   util-linux

/usr/bin	stdin	stdout	- file	-- opt	--help	--version

The chfn (change finger) command updates a few pieces of personal information maintained by the system: real name, home telephone, office telephone, and office location, as displayed by the finger command. Invoked without a username, chfn affects your account; invoked with a username (by root), it affects that user. With no options, chfn will prompt you for the desired information.

```
$ chfn
Password: ********
Name [Shawn Smith]: Shawn E. Smith
Office [100 Barton Hall]:
Office Phone [212-555-1212]: 212-555-1234
Home Phone []:
```

Useful options

-f *name*	Change the full name to *name*.
-h *phone*	Change the home phone number to *phone*.
-p *phone*	Change the office phone number to *phone*.
-o *office*	Change the office location to *office*.

chsh [*options*] [*username*]   util-linux

/usr/bin		stdin	**stdout**	- file	-- opt	--help	--version

The chsh (change shell) command sets your login shell program. Invoked without a username, chsh affects your account; invoked with a username (by root), it affects that user. With no options, chsh will prompt you for the desired information.

```
$ chsh
Changing shell for smith.
Password: ********
New shell [/bin/bash]: /bin/tcsh
```

The new shell must be listed in */etc/shells*.

Useful options

-s *shell*	Specify the new shell.
-l	List all permissible shells.

Becoming the Superuser

Normal users, for the most part, can modify only the files they own. One special user, called the *superuser* or *root*, has full access to the machine and can do anything on it. To become the superuser, log in as yourself and type:

```
$ su -l
Password: ********
#
```

You will be prompted for the superuser password (which we presume you know, if it's your computer). Your shell prompt will change to a hash mark (#) to indicate you are the superuser. When finished executing commands as the superuser, type ^D or run exit to end the superuser shell and become yourself again.

This is the simplest way to obtain superuser privileges on the system. There are other programs for doing so which offer more control, such as sudo, but they are beyond the scope of this book.

If you provide a username to su:

```
$ su -l jones
Password: ********
```

you can become that user (provided you know her password).

Useful options

-l	Run a login shell. You almost always want this option, so root's proper search path is set.
-m	Preserve your current environment variables in the new shell.
-c *command*	Run just this *command* (as the other user) and exit. If you need to do this a lot, read the sudo manpage.
-s *shell*	Run the given shell (e.g., */bin/bash*).

Working with Groups

groups	Print the group membership of a user
groupadd	Create a new group
groupdel	Delete a group
groupmod	Modify a group

A *group* is a set of user accounts treated as a single entity. If you give permission for a group to take some action (such as modify a file), then all members of that group can take it. For example, you can give full permissions for the group friends to read, write, and execute the file */tmp/sample*:

```
$ groups
users smith friends
```

```
$ chgrp friends /tmp/sample
$ chmod 770 /tmp/sample
$ ls -l /tmp/sample
-rwxrwx--- 1 smith friends 2874 Oct 20 22:35 /tmp/sample
```

To add users to a group, edit */etc/group* as root.* To change
the group ownership of a file, recall the chgrp commands
from "File Properties" on page 56.

groups [*usernames*]

coreutils

/usr/bin		stdin	**stdout**	- file	-- opt	--**help**	--**version**

The groups command prints the Linux groups to which you
belong, or to which other users belong:

```
$ whoami
smith
$ groups
smith users
$ groups jones root
jones : jones users
root : root bin daemon sys adm disk wheel src
```

groupadd [*options*] *group*

shadow-utils

/usr/sbin		stdin	stdout	- file	-- **opt**	--help	--version

The groupadd command creates a new group. In most cases, you
should use the -f option to prevent duplicate groups from being
created:

```
# groupadd -f friends
```

Useful options

-g *gid*   Specify your own numeric group ID instead of letting groupadd choose one.

-f   If the specified group exists already, complain and exit.

groupdel *group*

shadow-utils

/usr/sbin		stdin	stdout	- file	-- **opt**	--help	--version

The groupdel command deletes an existing group.

```
# groupdel friends
```

---

* Different systems may store the group member list in other ways.

Before doing this, it's a good idea to identify all files that have their group ID set to the given group, so you can deal with them later:

```
# find / -group friends -print
```

because groupdel does not change the group ownership of any files. It simply removes the group name from the system's records.

groupmod [*options*] *group*
shadow-utils

/usr/sbin	stdin	stdout	- file	-- opt	--help	--version

The groupmod command modifies the given group, changing its name or group ID.

```
# groupmod -n newname friends
```

groupmod does not affect any files owned by this group: it simply changes the ID or name in the system's records. Be careful when changing the ID, or these files will have their group ownership set to a nonexistent group.

Useful options

-g *gid*   Change the group's ID to *gid*.

-n *name*   Change the group's name to *name*.

Basic Host Information

uname	Print basic system information
hostname	Print the system's hostname
dnsdomainname	Same as hostname -d
domainname	Same as hostname -y
nisdomainname	Same as hostname -y
ypdomainname	Same as hostname -y
ifconfig	Set and display network interface information

Every Linux machine (or *host*) has a name, a network IP address, and other properties. Here's how to display this information.

uname [*options*]

coreutils

/bin	stdin	stdout	- file	-- opt	--help	--version

The uname command prints fundamental information about your computer:

```
$ uname -a
Linux server.example.com 2.4.18-27.8.0 #1 Fri Mar 14 06:
45:49 EST 2003 i686 i686 i386 GNU/Linux
```

This includes the kernel name (Linux), hostname (server.example. com), kernel version (2.4.18-27.8.0 #1 Fri Mar 14 06:45:49 EST 2003), hardware name (i686), processor type (i686), hardware platform (i386), and operating system name (GNU/Linux).

Useful options

-a	All information.
-s	Only the kernel name (the default).
-n	Only the hostname.
-r	Only the kernel version.
-m	Only the hardware name.
-p	Only the processor type.
-i	Only the hardware platform.
-o	Only the operating system name.

hostname [*options*] [*name*]

net-tools

/bin	stdin	stdout	- file	-- opt	--help	--version

The hostname command prints the name of your computer. Depending how you have things set up, this might be the fully-qualified hostname:

```
$ hostname
myhost.example.com
```

or your short hostname:

```
$ hostname
myhost
```

You can also set your hostname, as root:

```
# hostname orange
```

However, hostnames and nameservers are complicated topics well beyond the scope of this book. Don't just blindly start setting hostnames!

Useful options

-i	Print your host's IP address.
-a	Print your host's alias name.
-s	Print your host's short name.
-f	Print your host's fully-qualified name.
-d	Print your host's DNS domain name.
-y	Print your host's NIS or YP domain name.
-F *hostfile*	Set your hostname by reading the name from file *hostfile*.

ifconfig *interface*   net-tools

/sbin		stdin	**stdout**	- file	-- opt	--help	--version

The ifconfig command displays and sets various aspects of your computer's network interface. This topic is beyond the scope of the book, but we'll teach you a few tricks.

To display information about the default network interface (usually called *eth0*):

```
$ ifconfig eth0
eth0      Link encap:Ethernet  HWaddr 00:50:BA:48:4F:BA
          inet addr:192.168.0.10  Bcast:192.168.0.255
Mask:255.255.255.0
          UP BROADCAST RUNNING MULTICAST  MTU:1500
Metric:1
          RX packets:1955231 errors:0 dropped:0 overruns:0
frame:0
          TX packets:1314765 errors:0 dropped:0 overruns:0
carrier:0
          collisions:0 txqueuelen:100
          RX bytes:2320504831 (2213.0 Mb)  TX bytes:
152785756 (145.7 Mb)
          Interrupt:11 Base address:0x6000
```

This includes your MAC address (00:50:BA:48:4F:BA), your IP address (192.168.0.21), your netmask (255.255.255.0), and various other information. To view all loaded network interfaces, run:

```
$ ifconfig -a
```

If you're experienced with networking, see the ifconfig manpage to learn more.

Host Location

host	Look up hostnames, IP addresses, and DNS info
whois	Look up the registrants of Internet domains
ping	Check if a remote host is reachable
traceroute	View the network path to a remote host

When dealing with remote computers, you might want to know more about them. Who owns them? What are the IP addresses? Where on the network are they located?

host [*options*] *name* [*server*]   bind-utils

/usr/bin	stdin	**stdout**	- file	-- opt	--help	--version

The host command looks up the hostname or IP address of a remote machine by querying DNS.

```
$ host www.redhat.com
www.redhat.com has address 66.187.232.50
$ host 66.187.232.50
50.232.187.66.in-addr.arpa domain name pointer www.redhat.
com.
```

It can also find out much more:

```
$ host -a www.redhat.com
Trying "www.redhat.com"
;; ->>HEADER<<- opcode: QUERY, status: NOERROR, id: 50419
;; flags: qr rd ra; QUERY: 1, ANSWER: 1, AUTHORITY: 3,
ADDITIONAL: 3

;; QUESTION SECTION:
;www.redhat.com.        IN   ANY
```

```
;; ANSWER SECTION:
www.redhat.com.     196  IN  A  66.187.232.50

;; AUTHORITY SECTION:
redhat.com.     90535  IN  NS  ns2.redhat.com.
redhat.com.     90535  IN  NS  ns3.redhat.com.
redhat.com.     90535  IN  NS  ns1.redhat.com.

;; ADDITIONAL SECTION:
ns2.redhat.com.     143358  IN  A  66.187.224.210
ns3.redhat.com.     143358  IN  A  66.187.229.10
ns1.redhat.com.     143358  IN  A  66.187.233.210
```

but a full discussion of nameservers is beyond the scope of this
book. The final, optional "server" parameter lets you specify a
particular nameserver for the query. Here's one at *comcast.net*:

```
$ host www.redhat.com ns01.jdc01.pa.comcast.net
Using domain server:
Name: ns01.jdc01.pa.comcast.net
Address: 66.45.25.71#53
Aliases:
www.redhat.com has address 66.187.232.50
```

To see all options, type host by itself.

Useful options

-a   Display all available information.

-t   Choose the type of nameserver query: A, AXFR, CNAME, HINFO, KEY,
         MX, NS, PTR, SIG, SOA, and so on.
```
$ host -t MX redhat.com
redhat.com mail is handled by 20 mx2.redhat.com.
redhat.com mail is handled by 10 mx1.redhat.com.
```

If the host command doesn't do what you want, try dig, another
powerful DNS lookup utility. You might also encounter the
nslookup command, mostly obsolete these days but still found on
some Linux and Unix systems.

whois [*options*] *domain_name*   jwhois

/usr/bin		stdin	**stdout**	- file	-- opt	--help	--version

The whois command looks up the registration of an Internet
domain:

```
$ whois redhat.com
Registrant:
```

```
Red Hat, Inc. (REDHAT-DOM)
    P.O. Box 13588
    Research Triangle Park, NC 27709
 ...
```

These days, you'll see a few screensful of legal disclaimers from
the registrar before or after the real information appears.

Useful options

-h *registrar*   Perform the lookup at the given registrar's server. For example,
                  whois -h whois.networksolutions.com yahoo.com.

-p *port*   Query the given the TCP port instead of the default, 43 (the whois
                  service).

ping [*options*] *host*   iputils

/bin   stdin   **stdout**   - file   -- opt   --help   --version

The ping command tells you if a remote host is reachable. It sends
small packets (ICMP packets to be precise) to a remote host and
waits for responses.

```
$ ping google.com
PING google.com (216.239.37.100) from 192.168.0.10 :
56(84) bytes of data.
64 bytes from www.google.com (216.239.37.100): icmp_seq=0
ttl=49 time=32.390 msec
64 bytes from www.google.com (216.239.37.100): icmp_seq=1
ttl=49 time=24.208 msec
^C
--- google.com ping statistics ---
2 packets transmitted, 2 packets received, 0% packet loss
round-trip min/avg/max/mdev = 24.208/28.299/32.390/4.091 ms
```

Useful options

-c *N*   Ping at most *N* times.

-i *N*   Wait *N* seconds (default 1) between pings.

-n   Print IP addresses in the output, rather than hostnames.

traceroute [*options*] *host* [*packet_length*]   traceroute

/bin   stdin   stdout   - file   -- opt   --help   --version

The traceroute command prints the network path from your local
host to a remote host, and the time it takes for packets to traverse
the path.

```
$ traceroute yahoo.com
  1 server.example.com (192.168.0.20) 1.397 ms 1.973 ms
2.817 ms
  2  10.221.16.1 (10.221.16.1)  15.397 ms  15.973 ms
10.817 ms
  3  gbr2-p10.cb1ma.ip.att.net (12.123.40.190)  11.952 ms
11.720 ms  11.705 ms
  ...
  16 p6.www.dcn.yahoo.com (216.109.118.69) 24.757 ms
22.659 ms  *
```

Each host in the path is sent three "probes" and the return times
are reported. If a host does not respond within five seconds,
traceroute prints an asterisk. Also, traceroute may be blocked by
firewalls or unable to proceed for various reasons, in which case it
prints a symbol.

Symbol	Meaning
!F	Fragmentation needed.
!H	Host unreachable.
!N	Network unreachable.
!P	Protocol unreachable.
!S	Source route failed.
!X	Communication administratively prohibited.
!*N*	ICMP unreachable code *N*.

The default packet size is 40 bytes, but you can change this with
the final, optional *packet_length* parameter (e.g., traceroute
myhost 120).

Useful options

-n	Numeric mode: print IP addresses instead of hostnames.
-w N	Change the timeout from five seconds to N seconds.

Network Connections

ssh	Securely log into a remote host, or run commands on it
telnet	Log into a remote host (insecure!)
scp	Securely copy files to/from a remote host (batch)
sftp	Securely copy files to/from a remote host (interactive)
ftp	Copy files to/from a remote host (interactive, insecure!)

With Linux, it's easy to establish network connections from one machine to another for remote logins and file transfers. Just make sure you do it securely.

ssh [*options*] *host* [*command*]   openssh-clients

/usr/bin	stdin	stdout	- file	-- opt	--help	--version

The ssh (Secure Shell) program securely logs you into a remote machine where you already have an account:

```
$ ssh remote.example.com
```

Alternatively, it can invoke a program on that remote machine without logging you in:

```
$ ssh remote.example.com who
```

ssh encrypts all data that travels across its connection, including your username and password (which you'll need to access the remote machine). The SSH protocol also supports other ways to authenticate, such as public keys and host IDs. See man sshd for details.

Useful options

-l *username*	Specify your remote *username*; otherwise, ssh assumes your local username. You can also use the syntax *username@host*: $ ssh smith@server.example.com
-p *port*	Use a *port* number other than the default (22).
-t	Allocate a tty on the remote system; useful when trying to run a remote command with an interactive user interface, such as a text editor.
-v	Produce verbose output, useful for debugging.

telnet [*options*] *host* [*port*]   telnet

/usr/bin	stdin	**stdout**	- file	-- opt	--help	--version

The telnet program logs you into a remote machine where you already have an account.

```
$ telnet remote.example.com
```

Avoid telnet for remote logins: most implementations are insecure and send your password over the network in plain text for anyone to steal. Use ssh instead, which protects your password and data via encryption. There are two exceptions:

- In a Kerberos environment, using enhanced ("kerberized") Telnet software on both the client and server side). Fedora telnet can work with Kerberos. See *http://web.mit.edu/kerberos/* for more information.

- Connecting to a remote port when you aren't sending any sensitive information at all. For example, to check for the presence of a web server (port 80) on a remote system:

```
$ telnet remote.example.com 80
Trying 192.168.55.21...
Connected to remote.example.com (192.168.55.21).
Escape character is '^]'.
xxx            Type some junk and press Enter
<HTML><HEAD>  # Yep, it's a web server
<TITLE>400 Bad Request</TITLE>
</HEAD><BODY>
<H1>Bad Request</H1>
Your browser sent a request that
this server could not understand.<P>
</BODY></HTML>
Connection closed by foreign host.
```

To discourage you further from using telnet, we aren't even going to describe its options.

scp *local_spec remote_spec*
openssh-clients

/usr/bin   stdin   stdout   - file   -- opt   --help   --version

The scp (secure copy) command copies files and directories from one computer to another in batch. (For an interactive user interface, see sftp.) It encrypts all communication between the two machines.

```
$ scp myfile remote.example.com:newfile
$ scp -r mydir remote.example.com:
$ scp remote.example.com:myfile .
$ scp -r remote.example.com:mydir .
```

To specify an alternate username on the remote system, use the *username@host* syntax:

```
$ scp myfile smith@remote.example.com:
```

Useful options

-p   Duplicate all file attributes (permissions, timestamps) when copying.

-r   Recursively copy a directory and its contents.

-v   Produce verbose output, useful for debugging.

sftp (*host* | *username@host*)
openssh-clients

/usr/bin   stdin   stdout   - file   -- opt   --help   --version

The sftp program copies files interactively between two computers. (As opposed to scp, which copies files in batch.) The user interface is much like that of ftp.

```
$ sftp remote.example.com
Password: ********
sftp> cd MyFiles
sftp> ls
README
file1
file2
file3
sftp> get file2
Fetching /home/smith/MyFiles/file2 to file2
sftp> quit
```

If your username on the remote system is different from your local one, use the *username@host* argument:

```
$ sftp smith@remote.example.com
```

Command	Meaning
help	View a list of available commands.
ls lls	List the files in the current remote (ls) or local (lls) directory.
pwd lpwd	Print the remote (pwd) or local (lpwd) working directory.
cd *dir* lcd *dir*	Change your remote (cd) or local (lcd) directory to be *dir*.
get *file1* [*file2*]	Copy remote *file1* to local machine, optionally renamed as *file2*.
put *file1* [*file2*]	Copy local *file1* to remote machine, optionally renamed as *file2*.
mget *file**	Copy multiple remote files to the local machine using wildcards * and ?.
mput *file**	Copy multiple local files to the remote machine using wildcards * and ?.
quit	Exit sftp.

ftp [*options*] host   ftp

/usr/bin	stdin	stdout	- file	-- opt	--help	--version

The ftp (File Transfer Protocol) program copies files between computers, but not in a secure manner: your username and password travel over the network as plain text. Use sftp instead whenever possible.

The same commands we listed for sftp also work for ftp. (However, the two programs support other, differing commands, too.)

Email

evolution	GUI email client
mutt	Text-based mail client
mail	Minimal text-based mail client

Fedora includes a number of mail readers. We'll look at three with different purposes and strengths. Other Linux mailers include pine, the RMAIL and vm applications built into emacs, and mozilla's Mail & News.

To see the progress of email messages you send and receive, view the logfile */var/log/maillog*. As root, you can use the mailq command to view any outgoing mail messages still queued on your machine, waiting to be sent.

evolution

/usr/bin		stdin	stdout	- file	-- opt	**--help**	**--version**

Ximian Evolution is a graphical email program that looks a lot like Microsoft Outlook. Depending on how your system is set up, you can invoke Evolution from the main menu as Internet : Evolution Email, or by running the command evolution from the shell.

To set up a mail account:

1. Choose Tools → Settings...
2. In the Evolution Settings window, if you do not already have an email account listed, choose Add. Otherwise, select the account and choose Edit.
3. In the Evolution Account Editor window, the Identity tab, fill in your full name and email address.
4. Choose the Receiving Mail tab and the Server Type (IMAP, POP, local delivery, and so on) and fill in the fields relevant to your mail server. For POP or IMAP servers, fill in the mail server host and username supplied by your ISP; for local delivery, fill in the path to your local mailbox.
5. Choose the Sending Mail tab and select the type of your outgoing mail server: SMTP if the server is remote (you'll be

prompted for the hostname), or sendmail if the server is the local machine.

6. The rest of the tabs and options are at your discretion. Choose OK to exit the Evolution Account Editor. You should be ready for basic mail operations.

Inbox	View your mail
New	Compose a new mail message
Send/Receive	Check for new mail
Reply	Reply to a message, only to the sender
Reply To All	Reply to a message, to all addresses in the To and CC lines
Forward	Forward a message to a third party

There are many more features—experiment!

mutt [*options*]   mutt

/usr/bin   stdin   stdout   - file   -- opt   --help   --version

mutt is a text-based mailer that runs in an ordinary terminal (or terminal window), so it can be used both locally (e.g., in an X terminal window) or remotely over an SSH connection. It is very powerful, with many commands and options. To invoke it, type:

    $ mutt

When the main screen appears, any messages in your mailbox are listed briefly, one per line. The commands in Table 4 are available.

Table 4. mutt commands available on the main screen

Keystroke	Meaning
Up arrow	Move to the previous message.
Down arrow	Move to the next message.
PageUp	Scroll up one pageful of messages.
PageDown	Scroll down one pageful of messages.
Home	Move to the first message.
End	Move to the last message.
m	Compose a new mail message. This invokes your default text editor. After editing the message and exiting the editor, type y to send the message or q to postpone it.

Table 4. mutt commands available on the main screen (continued)

Keystroke	Meaning
r	Reply to current message. Works like m.
f	Forward the current message to a third party. Works like m.
i	View the contents of your mailbox.
C	Copy the current message to another mailbox.
d	Delete the current message.

While writing a message, after you exit your text editor, the commands in Table 5 are available.

Table 5. mutt commands available while writing a message

Keystroke	Meaning
a	Attach a file (an attachment) to the message.
c	Set the CC list.
b	Set the BCC list.
e	Edit the message again.
r	Edit the Reply-To field.
s	Edit the subject line.
y	Send the message.
C	Copy the message to a file.
q	Postpone the message without sending it.

The commands in Table 6 are always available.

Table 6. Other mutt commands

Keystroke	Meaning
?	See a list of all commands (type SPACEBAR to scroll down, q to quit).
^G	Cancel the command in progress.
q	Quit.

The official mutt site is *http://www.mutt.org*, and there's a short mutt tutorial at *http://www.cs.utk.edu/~help/mail/mutt_starting.php*.

mail [*options*] *recipient* MailX

/bin		stdin	stdout	- file	-- opt	--help	--version

The mail program (equivalently, Mail)[*] is a quick, simple email client. Most people want a more powerful program for regular use, but for quick messages from the command line or in scripts, mail is really handy.

To send a quick message:

```
$ mail smith@example.com
Subject: my subject
I'm typing a message.
To end it, I type a period by itself on a line.
.
Cc: jones@example.com
$
```

To send a quick message using a single command:

```
$ echo "Hello world" | mail -s "subject" smith@example.com
```

To mail a file using a single command, use either of these:

```
$ mail -s "my subject" smith@example.com < filename
$ cat filename | mail -s "my subject" smith@example.com
```

Notice how easily you can send the output of a pipeline as an email message.

Useful options

-s *subject*	Set the subject line of an outgoing message.
-v	Verbose mode: print messages about mail delivery.
-c *addresses*	CC the message to the given addresses, a comma-separated list.
-b *addresses*	BCC the message to the given addresses, a comma-separated list.

---

[*] On older Unix systems, Mail and mail were rather different programs, but on Linux they are the same: */usr/bin/Mail* is a symbolic link to */bin/mail*.

Web Browsing

mozilla	Full-featured web browser
lynx	Text-only web browser
wget	Retrieve web pages to disk
curl	Retrieve web pages to disk

Linux offers several ways to explore the World Wide Web: traditional browsers, text-based browsers, and page-retrieval utilities.

mozilla [*options*] [*URL*]   mozilla

/usr/bin		stdin	stdout	- file	-- opt	--help	--version

Mozilla is one of the most popular web browsers for Linux; it runs on most other operating systems as well, including an X window. Start it in the background with:

```
$ mozilla &
```

Mozilla provides features you'd expect (browsing, forward and back buttons, bookmarks, history, and so on), plus tabbed browsing, pop-up window suppression, and much, much more. It also has a full-featured email program and Usenet news reader. In the Help menu, select Help Contents to get started, and visit *http://www.mozilla.org* for full information.

Some other web browsers for Linux include Firebird (a stripped-down Mozilla, *http://www.mozilla.org/products/firebird*), Netscape (based on the same engine as Mozilla, *http://www.netscape.com*), Opera (*http://www.opera.com*), Konquerer for KDE (*http://www.konquerer.org*), Epiphany for GNOME (*http://www.gnome.org*), and Galeon (also based on Mozilla, *http://galeon.sourceforge.net*).

lynx [*options*] [*URL*]   lynx

/usr/bin		stdin	stdout	- file	-- opt	--help	--version

lynx is a text-only web browser: a rarity these days, but quite useful when graphics don't matter, or over slow network connections.

```
$ lynx http://www.yahoo.com
```

All browsing is done by keyboard, not mouse. Many pages will not look quite right, especially if they use tables or frames extensively, but usually you can find your way around a site.

Keystroke	Meaning
?	Get help.
k	List all keystrokes and their meanings.
^G	Cancel a command in progress.
q	Quit lynx.
Enter	"Click" the current link, or finish the current form field.
Left arrow	Back to previous page.
Right arrow	Forward to next page, or "click" the current link.
g	Go to a URL (you'll be prompted to enter it).
p	Save, print, or mail the current page.
Spacebar	Scroll down.
b	Scroll up.
Down arrow	Go to the next link or form field.
Up arrow	Go to the previous link or form field.
^A	Go to top of page.
^E	Go to end of page.
m	Return to the main/home page.
/	Search for text on the page.
a	Bookmark the current page.
v	View your bookmark list.
r	Delete a bookmark.
=	Display properties of the current page and link.
\	View HTML source (type again to return to normal view).

lynx has over 100 command-line options, so the manpage is well worth exploring.

Useful options

-dump	Print the rendered page to standard output and exit. (Compare to -source.)
-source	Print the HTML source to standard output and exit. (Compare to the wget and curl commands.)
-emacskeys	Make lynx obey keystrokes reminiscent of the emacs editor.
-vikeys	Make lynx obey keystrokes reminiscent of the vim (or vi) editor.
-homepage=URL	Set your home page URL to be URL.
-color -nocolor	Turn colored text mode on and off.

wget [*options*] URL   wget

/usr/bin   stdin stdout - file -- opt --help --version

The wget command hits a URL and downloads the information to a file or standard output. It's great for capturing individual pages or entire web page hierarchies to arbitrary depth. For example, let's capture the Yahoo home page:

```
$ wget http://www.yahoo.com
--23:19:51--  http://www.yahoo.com/
           => `index.html'
Resolving www.yahoo.com... done.
Connecting to www.yahoo.com[216.109.118.66]:80...
connected.
HTTP request sent, awaiting response... 200 OK
Length: unspecified [text/html]

    [ <=>                                    ] 31,434
220.84K/s

23:19:51 (220.84 KB/s) - `index.html' saved [31434]
```

which is saved to a file *index.html* in the current directory. wget has the added ability to resume a download if it gets interrupted in the middle, say, due to a network failure: just run wget -c with the same URL and it picks up where it left off.

Another similar command is curl, which writes to standard output by default—unlike wget, which duplicates the original page filenames by default.

```
$ curl http://www.yahoo.com > mypage.html
```

---

wget has over 70 options, so we'll cover just a few important ones. (curl has a different set of options; see its manpage.)

Useful options

-i *filename*	Read URLs from the given file and retrieve them in turn.
-O *filename*	Write all the captured HTML to the given file, one page appended after the other.
-c	Continue mode: if a previous retrieval was interrupted, leaving only a partial file as a result, pick up where wget left off. That is, if wget had downloaded 100K of a 150K file, the -c option says to retrieve only the remaining 50K and append it to the existing file. wget can be fooled, however, if the remote file has changed since the first (partial) download, so use this option only if you know the remote file hasn't changed.
-t N	Try *N* times before giving up. *N*=0 means try forever.
--progress=dot --progress=bar	Print dots or bars to show the download progress.
--spider	Don't do any downloading, just check the existence of the remote pages.
-nd	Retrieve all files into the current directory, even if remotely they are in a more complex directory tree. (By default, wget duplicates the remote directory hierarchy.)
-r	Retrieve a page hierarchy recursively: all directories and subdirectories.
-l N	Retrieve files at most *N* levels deep (5 by default).
-k	In all retrieved files, modify links so pages can be viewed locally.
-p	Download all necessary files to make a page display completely, such as stylesheets and images.
-L	Follow relative links (within a page) but not absolute links.
-A *pattern1,pattern2, pattern3,...*	Accept mode: download only files whose names match a given pattern. Patterns may contain the same wildcards as the shell.
-R *pattern1,pattern2, pattern3,...*	Reject mode: download only files whose names *do not* match a given pattern.

`-I pattern1,pattern2, pattern3,...`	Directory inclusion: download files only from directories that match a given pattern.
`-X`	Directory exclusion: download files only from directories that *do not* match a given pattern.

Usenet News

Usenet News is one of the oldest communities online today. It consists of tens of thousands of *newsgroups*, discussion forums in which people post (submit) messages and reply to them. Fedora includes the newsreader slrn, but there are dozens more available on the Net (rn, trn, tin, and so on). Mozilla also can read Usenet News: from the Window menu choose Mail & Newsgroups. Usenet News can also be searched at Google Groups, *http://groups.google.com*.

In order to access Usenet, you need to connect to a news server, an Internet host that permits reading and posting of news articles. Once you can connect to a news server (say, *news.example.com*), a record of your subscribed newsgroups and which articles you've read is kept in a file in your home directory automatically. Depending on your newsreader configuration, the file is either *~/.newsrc* or *~/.jnewsrc*.

slrn [*options*]   slrn

/usr/bin	stdin	stdout	- file	-- opt	--help	--version

slrn is a Usenet newsreader. Before using it, you must specify a news server by setting your shell's NNTPSERVER variable:

```
$ export NNTPSERVER=news.example.com
```

Then create a newsgroups file (only if you haven't used slrn on this computer before):

```
$ slrn --create
```

and start reading news:

```
$ slrn
```

When invoked, slrn displays the News Groups page with a list of your subscribed newsgroups. Table 7 shows some useful commands.

Table 7. Usenet slrn keystrokes for newsgroups

Keystroke	Meaning
q	Quit slrn.
Down	Select next newsgroup.
Up	Select previous newsgroup.
Enter	Read the selected newsgroup.
p	Post a new article in the selected newsgroup.
a	Add a new newsgroup (you must know the name).
u	Unsubscribe from the selected newsgroup (it will be removed after you quit). Type s to resubscribe.

When you press Enter to read a newsgroup, slrn displays a Group page, containing the available discussions (or "threads") in that newsgroup. Table 8 shows the useful commands on this page.

Table 8. Useful slrn commands for managing discussion threads

Keystroke	Meaning
q	Quit and go back to the News Groups page.
Down	Select next thread.
Up	Select previous thread.
Enter	Begin reading the selected thread.
c	Mark all threads as read ("catch up"): type ESCAPE u to undo.

Table 9 lists some commands you can use while reading an article.

Table 9. Useful slrn commands for reading articles

Keystroke	Meaning
q	Quit reading and return to the Group page.
Spacebar	Go to next page of article.
b	Go back to previous page of article.

Table 9. Useful slrn commands for reading articles (continued)

Keystroke	Meaning
r	Reply to the author by email.
f	Post a followup article.
P	Post a new article.
o	Save the article in a file.
n	Go to next unread article.
p	Go to previous unread article.

At any time you can type ? for the help page. slrn has a tremendous number of commands and options, and can be configured via the file ~/.slrnrc. We've covered only the basics; see */usr/share/doc/slrn** and *http://www.slrn.org* for more information.

Instant Messaging

gaim	Instant messaging and IRC client
talk	Linux/Unix chat program
write	Send messages to a terminal
mesg	Prohibit talk and write
tty	Print your terminal device name

Linux provides various ways to send messages to other users on the same machine or elsewhere on the Internet. These range from the ancient programs talk and write, which work over Linux terminal devices (ttys), to more modern Instant Messaging clients like gaim.

gaim [*options*]   gaim

/usr/bin   stdin   stdout   - file   -- opt   --help   --version

gaim is a instant messaging client that works with many different protocols, including AOL, MSN, Yahoo, and more. It is also an IRC (Internet Relay Chat) client. It runs in an X window:

```
$ gaim &
```

If you don't already have an account with one of these IM services, you'll need to create one first; for example, visit *http://www.aim.com* to create an AOL Instant Messenger account. Once this is done, simply click the Accounts button to indicate your account to gaim, enter your screen name and password in the login window, and you should be connected.

Useful options

-u *screenname*   Set your default account to be *screenname*.

-l   Automatically log in when invoking gaim (assuming your password is stored).

-w [*message*]   Set yourself to be away, with an optional away *message*.

talk [*user*[*@host*]] [*tty*]   talk

/usr/bin	stdin	stdout	- file	-- opt	--help	--version

The talk program predates modern instant messaging by a few decades: it connects two users, logged in on the same or different hosts, for one-to-one communication. It's supplied on Linux and Unix machines (and has been ported to other platforms) and runs in a text window such as an xterm. It splits the window horizontally so you can see your own typing and that of your partner.

```
$ talk friend@example.com
```

If your partner is logged in multiple times, you can specify one of his ttys for the talk connection.

write *user* [*tty*]   util-linux

/usr/bin	stdin	stdout	- file	-- opt	--help	--version

The write program is more primitive than talk: it sends lines of text from one logged-in user to another on the same Linux machine.

```
$ write smith
Hi, how are you?
See you later.
^D
```

^D ends the connection. write is also useful in pipelines for quick one-off messages:

```
$ echo 'Howdy!' | write smith
```

mesg [y|n]
SysVinit

/usr/bin   stdin   stdout   - file   -- opt   --help   --version

The `mesg` program controls whether `talk` and `write` connections can reach your terminal. `mesg y` permits them, `mesg n` denies them, and `mesg` prints the current status (y or n).* `mesg` has no effect on modern instant messaging programs like `gaim`.

```
$ mesg
is n
$ mesg y
```

tty
coreutils

/usr/bin   stdin   stdout   - file   -- opt   --help   --version

The `tty` program prints the name of the terminal device associated with the current shell.

```
$ tty
/dev/pts/4
```

Screen Output

echo	Print simple text on standard output
printf	Print formatted text on standard output
yes	Print repeated text on standard output
seq	Print a sequence of numbers on standard output
clear	Clear the screen or window

Linux provides several commands for printing messages on standard output, in case you like to talk to yourself:

```
$ echo hello world
hello world
```

Each command has different strengths and intended purposes. These commands are invaluable for learning about

---

* At press time, `mesg y` on Fedora fails with the error message, "tty device is not owned by group 'tty'." We expect this problem will get sorted out.

Linux, debugging problems, and writing shell scripts (see "Programming with Shell Scripts" on page 166).

echo [*options*] *strings* bash

shell built-in	stdin	**stdout**	- file	-- opt	--help	--version

The echo command simply prints its arguments:

```
$ echo We are having fun
We are having fun
```

Unfortunately, there are several different echo commands with slightly different behavior. There's */bin/echo*, but Linux shells typically override this with a built-in command called echo. To find out which you're using, run the command type echo.

Useful options

-n	Don't print a final newline character.
-e	Recognize and interpret escape characters. For example, try echo 'hello\a' and echo -e 'hello\a'. The first prints literally and the second makes a beep.
-E	Don't interpret escape characters: the opposite of -e.

Available escape characters are listed below.

\a	Alert (play a beep)
\b	Backspace
\c	Don't print the final newline (same effect as -n)
\f	Form feed
\n	Line feed (newline)
\r	Carriage return
\t	Horizontal tab
\v	Vertical tab
\\	A backslash
\'	Single quote
\"	Double quote
\nnn	The character whose ASCII value is *nnn* in octal

printf *format_string* [*arguments*] bash

The printf command is an enhanced echo: it prints formatted strings on standard output. It operates much like the C programming language function printf( ), which applies a format string to a sequence of arguments to create some specified output. For example:

```
$ printf "User %s is %d years old.\n" sandy 29
User sandy is 29 years old.
```

The first argument is the format string, which in our example contains two format specifications, %s and %d. The subsequent arguments, sandy and 29, are substituted by printf into the format string, and then printed. Format specifications can get fancy with floating-point numbers:

```
$ printf "That\'ll be $%0.2f, sir.\n" 3
That'll be $3.00, sir.
```

There are two printf commands available in Linux: one built into the bash shell, and one in */usr/bin/printf*. The two are identical except for one format specification, %q, supported only by the bash built-in: it prints escape symbols ("\") so its output can be used as shell input safely. Note the difference:

```
$ printf "This is a quote: %s\n" "\""
This is a quote: "
$ printf "This is a quote: %q\n" "\""
This is a quote: \"
```

It is your responsibility to make sure the number of format specifications equals the number of arguments supplied to printf. If you have too many arguments, the extras are ignored, and if you have too few, printf assumes default values (0 for numeric formats, "" for string formats). Nevertheless, you should treat such mismatches as errors, even though printf is forgiving. If they lurk in your shell scripts, they are bugs waiting to happen.

Format specifications are described in detail on the manpage for the C function printf (see man 3 printf). Here are some useful ones.

%d	Decimal integer
%ld	Long decimal integer
%o	Octal integer
%x	Hexadecimal integer

%f	Floating point
%lf	Double-precision floating point
%c	A single character
%s	String
%q	String with any shell metacharacters escaped
%%	A percent sign by itself

Just after the leading percent sign, you can insert a numeric expression for the minimum width of the output. For example, "%5d" means to print a decimal number in a five-character-wide field, and "%6.2f" means a floating-point number in a six-character-wide field with two digits after the decimal point. Some useful numeric expressions are:

n	Minimum width n.
$0n$	Minimum width n, padded with leading zeroes.
$n.m$	Minimum width n, with m digits after the decimal point.

printf also interprets escape characters like "\n" (print a newline character) and "\a" (ring the bell). See the echo command for the full list.

yes [*string*] coreutils

/usr/bin   stdin   **stdout**   - file   -- opt   **--help**   **--version**

The yes command prints the given string (or "y" by default) forever, one string per line.

```
$ yes again
again
again
again
...
```

Though it might seem useless at first glance, yes can be perfect for turning interactive commands into batch commands. Want to get rid of an annoying "Are you SURE you want to do that" message? Pipe the output of yes into the input of the command to answer all those prompts:

```
$ yes | my_interactive_command
```

When *my_interactive_command* terminates, so will yes.

seq [*options*] *specification*

/usr/bin   stdin **stdout**   - file   -- opt   **--help**   **--version**

The seq command prints a sequence of integers or real numbers, suitable for piping to other programs. There are three kinds of specification arguments:

A single number: an upper limit
seq begins at 1 and counts up or down to the number.

```
$ seq 3
1
2
3
```

Two numbers: lower and upper limit
seq begins at the first number and counts as far as it can without passing the second number.

```
$ seq 5 2
5
4
3
2
```

Three numbers: lower limit, increment, and upper limit
seq begins at the first number, increments by the second number, and stops at (or before) the third number.

```
$ seq 1 .3 2
1
1.3
1.6
1.9
```

Useful options

-w
Print leading zeroes, as necessary, to give all lines the same width:
```
$ seq -w 8 10
08
09
10
```

-f *format_string*
Format the output lines with a printf-like format string, which must include either %g (the default), %e, or %f:
```
$ seq -f '**%g**' 3
**1**
**2**
**3**
```

-s *string*	Use the given string as a separator between the numbers. By default, a newline is printed (i.e., one number per line):

```
$ seq -s ':' 10
1:2:3:4:5:6:7:8:9:10
```

clear
ncurses

/usr/bin	stdin	**stdout**	- file	-- opt	--help	--version

This command simply clears your display or shell window.

Math and Calculations

xcalc	Display a graphical calculator
expr	Evaluate simple math on the command line
dc	Text-based calculator

Need a calculator? Linux provides not only a familiar graphical calculator, but also some command-line programs to compute mathematical truths for you.

xcalc [*options*]
XFree86-tools

/usr/X11R6/bin	stdin	stdout	- file	-- opt	--help	--version

The xcalc command displays a simple, graphical calculator in an X window. The default is a traditional calculator; if you prefer a reverse-polish notation (RPN) calculator, supply the -rpn option.

expr *expression*
coreutils

/usr/bin	stdin	**stdout**	- file	-- opt	**--help**	**--version**

The expr command does simple math (and other expression evaluation) on the command line:

```
$ expr 7 + 3
10
$ expr '(' 7 + 3 ')' '*' 14      Special shell characters are quoted
140
$ expr length ABCDEFG
7
$ expr 15 '>' 16
0
```

Each argument must be separated by whitespace. Notice we had to quote or escape any characters that have special meaning to the shell. Parentheses (escaped) may be used for grouping. Table 10 lists operators for expr.

Table 10. Operators for expr

Operator	Numeric operation	String operation
+	Addition	
-	Subtraction	
*	Multiplication	
/	Integer division	
%	Remainder (modulo)	
<	Less than	Earlier in dictionary
<=	Less than or equal	Earlier in dictionary, or equal
>	Greater than	Later in dictionary
>=	Greater than or equal	Later in dictionary, or equal
=	Equality	Equality
!=	Inequality	Inequality
|	Boolean "or"	Boolean "or"
&	Boolean "and"	Boolean "and"
s : *regexp*		Does the regular expression *regexp* match string *s*?
substr *s p n*		Print *n* characters of string *s*, beginning at position *p*. (*p*=1 is the first character.)
index *s chars*		Return the index of the first position in string *s* containing a character from string *chars*. Return 0 if not found. Same behavior as the C function index( ).

For Boolean expressions, the number 0 and the empty string are considered false; any other value is true. For Boolean results, 0 is false and 1 is true.

expr is not very efficient. For more complex needs, consider using a language like Perl instead.

The dc (desk calculator) command is a reverse-polish notation (RPN), stack-based calculator that reads expressions from standard input and writes results to standard output. If you know how to use a Hewlett-Packard RPN calculator, dc is pretty easy to use once you understand its syntax. But if you're used to traditional calculators, dc may seem inscrutable. We'll cover only some basic commands.

For stack and calculator operations:

q	Quit dc.
f	Print the entire stack.
c	Delete (clear) the entire stack.
p	Print the topmost value on the stack.
P	Pop (remove) the topmost value from the stack.
*n*k	Set precision of future operations to be *n* decimal places (default is 0: integer operations).

To pop the top two values from the stack, perform a requested operation, and push the result:

+	Addition.
-	Subtraction.
*	Multiplication.
/	Division.
%	Remainder.
^	Exponentiation (second-to-top value is the base, top value is the exponent).

To pop the top value from the stack, perform a requested operation, and push the result:

v	Square root.

Examples:

```
$ dc
4 5 + p          Print the sum of 4 and 5
9
```

2 3 ^ p	*Raise 2 to the 3rd power and print the result*
8	
10 * p	*Multiply the stack top by 10 and print the result*
80	
f	*Print the stack*
80	
9	
+p	*Pop the top two stack values and print their sum*
89	

Dates and Times

xclock	Display a graphical clock
cal	Print a calendar
date	Print or set the date and time
ntpdate	Set the system time using a remote timeserver

Need a date? How about a good time? Try these programs to display and set dates and times on your system.

xclock [*options*]   XFree86-tools

/usr/X11R6/bin	stdin	stdout	- file	-- opt	--help	--version

The xclock command displays a simple, graphical clock in an X window. If you prefer a different style, there are other clock programs included, such as oclock (round), t3d (3-D bouncing balls, located outside your search path in */usr/X11R6/lib/xscreensaver/t3d*), and the taskbar clocks displayed by GNOME and KDE.

Useful options

-analog	An analog clock with hands.
-digital [-brief]	A digital clock with full date and time; add -brief to show only the time.
-update *N*	Update the time display every *N* seconds.

cal [*options*] [*month* [*year*]]   util-linux

/usr/bin   stdin   **stdout**   - file   -- opt   --**help**   --version

The cal command prints a calendar—by default, the current month:

```
$ cal
   September 2003
Su Mo Tu We Th Fr Sa
    1  2  3  4  5  6
 7  8  9 10 11 12 13
14 15 16 17 18 19 20
21 22 23 24 25 26 27
28 29 30
```

To print a different calendar, supply a month and four-digit year: cal
8 2002. If you omit the month (cal 2002), the entire year is printed.

Useful options

-y   Print the current year's calendar.

-m   Business-week calendar: Make Monday the leftmost day.

-j   Number each day by its position in the year; in our example, September 1
           would be displayed as 244, September 2 as 245, and so on.

date [*options*] [*format*]   coreutils

/bin   stdin   **stdout**   - file   -- opt   --**help**   --version

The date command prints dates and times. By default, it prints the
system date and time in the local timezone:

```
$ date
Sun Sep 28 21:01:31 EDT 2003
```

You can format the output differently by supplying a format string
beginning with a plus sign:

```
$ date '+%D'
09/28/03
$ date '+The time is %l:%M %p on a beautiful %A in %B'
The time is  9:01 PM on a beautiful Sunday in September
```

Format	Meaning	Example
Whole dates and times:		
%c	Full date and time, 12-hour clock	Sun 28 Sep 2003, 09:01:25 PM EDT
%D	Numeric date, 2-digit year	09/28/03
%x	Numeric date, 4-digit year	09/28/2003
%T	Time, 24-hour clock	21:01:25

Format	Meaning	Example
%X	Time, 12-hour clock	09:01:25 PM
Words:		
%a	Day of week (abbreviated)	Sun
%A	Day of week (complete)	Sunday
%b	Month name (abbreviated)	Sep
%B	Month name (complete)	September
%Z	Time zone	EDT
%p	AM or PM	PM
Numbers:		
%w	Day of week (0–6, 0=Sunday)	0
%u	Day of week (1–7, 1=Monday)	7
%d	Day of month, leading zero	02
%e	Day of month, leading blank	2
%j	Day of year, leading zeroes	005
%m	Month number, leading zero	09
%y	Year, 2 digits	03
%Y	Year, 4 digits	2003
%M	Minute, leading zero	09
%S	Seconds, leading zero	05
%l	Hour, 12-hour clock, leading blank	9
%I	Hour, 12-hour clock, leading zero	09
%k	Hour, 24-hour clock, leading blank	9
%H	Hour, 24-hour clock, leading zero	09
%N	Nanoseconds	737418000
%s	Seconds since the beginning of Linux time: midnight January 1, 1970	1068583983
Other:		
%n	Newline	
%t	Tab	
%%	Percent sign	%

Through its options, date can also display other dates and times.

Useful options

-d *date_or_time_string*	Display the given *date_or_time_string*, formatted as you wish.
-r *filename*	Display the last-modified timestamp of the given file, formatted as you wish.
-s *date_or_time_string*	Set the system date and/or time; only the superuser can do this.

ntpdate *timeserver* ntp

/usr/sbin	stdin	**stdout**	- file	-- **opt**	--help	--version

The ntpdate command sets the current system time by contacting a timeserver machine on the network. You must be root to set the system time.

```
# /usr/sbin/ntpdate timeserver.someplace.edu
  7 Sep 21:01:25 ntpdate[2399]: step time server 178.99.1.8
offset 0.51 sec
```

To keep your system date in sync with a timeserver over long periods, use the daemon ntpd instead; see *http://www.ntp.org*. If you don't know a local timeserver, search Google for "public ntp time server".

Scheduling Jobs

sleep	Wait a set number of seconds, doing nothing
watch	Run a program at set intervals
at	Schedule a job for a single, future time
crontab	Schedule jobs for many future times

If you need to launch programs at particular times or at regular intervals, Linux provides several scheduling tools at various degrees of complexity.

sleep *time_specification* coreutils

/bin		stdin	stdout	- file	-- opt	--help	--version

The sleep command simply waits a set amount of time. The given time specification can be an integer (meaning seconds) or an integer followed by the letter s (also seconds), m (minutes), h (hours), or d (days).

```
$ sleep 5m                           Do nothing for 5 minutes
```

sleep is useful for delaying a command for a set amount of time:

```
$ sleep 10 && echo 'Ten seconds have passed.'
(10 seconds pass)
Ten seconds have passed.
```

watch [*options*] *command* procps

/usr/bin		stdin	**stdout**	- file	-- **opt**	--**help**	--**version**

The watch program executes a given command at regular intervals; the default is every two seconds. The command is passed to the shell (so be sure to quote or escape any special characters), and the results are displayed in a full-screen mode, so you can observe the output conveniently and see what has changed. For example, watch -n 60 date executes the date command once a minute, sort of a poor man's clock. Type ^C to exit.

Useful options

-n *seconds* Set the time between executions, in seconds.

-d   Highlight differences in the output, to emphasize what has changed from one execution to the next.

at [*options*] *time_specification* at

/usr/bin		stdin	**stdout**	- file	-- **opt**	--help	--version

The at command runs a shell command once at a specified time:

```
$ at 7am next sunday
at> echo Remember to go shopping | Mail smith
at> lpr $HOME/shopping-list
at> ^D
<EOT>
job 559 at 2003-09-14 21:30
```

The time specifications understood by at are enormously flexible. In general, you can specify:

- A time followed by a date (not a date followed by a time)
- Only a date (assumes the current clock time)
- Only a time (assumes the very next occurrence, whether today or tomorrow)
- A special word like now, midnight, or teatime (16:00)
- Any of the above followed by an offset, like "+ 3 days"

Dates are acceptable in many forms: december 25 2003, 25 december 2003, december 25, 25 december, 12/25/2003, 25.12.2003, 20031225, today, thursday, next thursday, next month, next year, and more. Month names can be abbreviated to three letters (jan, feb, mar, ...). Times are also flexible: 8pm, 8 pm, 8:00pm, 8:00 pm, 20:00, and 2000 are equivalent. Offsets are a plus or minus sign followed by whitespace and an amount of time: + 3 seconds, + 2 weeks, - 1 hour, and so on.[*]

If you don't specify a part of the date or time, at copies the missing information from the system date and time. So "next year" means one year from right now, "thursday" means the upcoming Thursday at the current clock time, "december 25" means the next upcoming December 25, and "4:30pm" means the very next occurrence of 4:30 p.m. in the future.

Your command is not evaluated by the shell until execution time, so wildcards, variables, and other shell constructs are not expanded until then. Also, your current environment (see printenv) is preserved within each job so it executes as if you were logged in. Aliases, however, aren't available to at jobs, so don't include them.

To list your at jobs, use atq ("at queue"):

```
$ atq
559   2003-09-14 07:00 a smith
```

To delete an at job, run atrm ("at remove") with the job number:

```
$ atrm 559
```

Useful options

-f *filename*   Read commands from the given file instead of standard input.

-c *job_number* Print the job commands to standard output.

---

[*] Programmers can read the precise syntax in */usr/share/doc/at-*/timespec*.

crontab [*options*] [*file*]

/usr/bin   stdin   stdout   - file   -- opt   --help   --version

The crontab command, like at, schedules jobs for specific times. However, crontab is for recurring jobs, such as "Run this command at midnight on the second Tuesday of each month." To make this work, you edit and save a file (called your *crontab file*):

```
$ crontab -e
```

which automatically gets installed in a system directory (*/var/ spool/cron*). Once a minute, a Linux process called cron wakes up, checks your crontab file, and executes any jobs that are due.

```
$ crontab -e
```
Edit your crontab file in your default editor ($EDITOR)

```
$ crontab -l
```
Print your crontab file on standard output

```
$ crontab -r
```
Delete your crontab file

```
$ crontab myfile
```
Install the file *myfile* as your crontab file

The superuser can add the option -u *username* to work with other users' crontab files.

Crontab files contain one job per line. (Blank lines and comment lines beginning with "#" are ignored.) Each line has six fields, separated by whitespace. The first five fields specify the time to run the job, and the last is the job command itself.

Minutes of the hour

Integers between 0 and 59. This can be a single number (30), a sequence of numbers separated by commas (0,15,30,45), a range (20–30), a sequence of ranges (0-15,50-59), or an asterisk to mean "all." You can also specify "every *n*th time" with the suffix /*n*; for instance, both */12 and 0-59/12 mean 0,12,24,36,48 (i.e., every 12 minutes).

Hours of the day

Same syntax as for minutes.

Days of the month

Integers between 1 and 31; again, you may use sequences, ranges, sequences of ranges, or an asterisk.

Months of the year

Integers between 1 and 12; again, you may use sequences, ranges, sequences of ranges, or an asterisk. Additionally, you may use three-letter abbreviations (jan, feb, mar, ...), but not in ranges or sequences.

Days of the week

Integers between 0 (Sunday) and 6 (Saturday); again, you may use sequences, ranges, sequences of ranges, or an asterisk. Additionally, you may use three-letter abbreviations (sun, mon, tue, ...), but not in ranges or sequences.

Command to execute

Any shell command, which will be executed in your login environment, so you can refer to environment variables like $HOME and expect them to work. Use only absolute paths to your commands (e.g., */usr/bin/who* instead of who) as a general rule.

Table 11 shows some example time specifications.

Table 11. Example time specifications for crontab

* * * * *	Every minute
45 * * * *	45 minutes after each hour (1:45, 2:45, etc.)
45 9 * * *	Every day at 9:45 am
45 9 8 * *	The eighth day of every month at 9:45 am
45 9 8 12 *	Every December 8 at 9:45 am
45 9 8 dec *	Every December 8 at 9:45 am
45 9 * * 6	Every Saturday at 9:45 am
45 9 * * sat	Every Saturday at 9:45 am
45 9 * 12 6	Every Saturday in December, at 9:45 am
45 9 8 12 6	Every December 8 AND every Saturday, at 9:45 am

If the command produces any output upon execution, cron will email it to you.

Graphics and Screensavers

eog	Display graphics files
gqview	Display graphics files and slideshows
ksnapshot	Take a screenshot (screen capture)
gimp	Edit graphics files
gnuplot	Create graphs and plots
xscreensaver	Run a screensaver

For viewing or editing graphics, Linux has handy tools with tons of options. We won't cover these programs in much detail, just enough to pique your interest. Our goal is to make you aware of the programs so you can explore further on your own.

eog [*options*] [*files*]
eog

/usr/bin	stdin	stdout	- file	-- opt	--help	--version

The eog (Eye of Gnome) image viewer displays graphics files in a variety of formats. If you invoke it for a single file, it displays the file. Invoked on two or more files:

```
$ eog file1.jpg file2.gif file3.pbm
```

it displays each in a separate window.

Most eog options are fairly technical, so we won't cover them; we mention this so you know eog *has* options, in case you want to investigate them (eog --help).

gqview [*options*] [*file*]
gqview

/usr/bin	stdin	stdout	- file	-- opt	--help	--version

The gqview image viewer displays graphics files in a variety of formats, and can automatically switch from one image to the next, like a slideshow. By default, it displays the names of all graphics files in the current directory, and you can select names to display the images. The onscreen menus are straightforward, so explore them and try things out. Type ^q to quit.

Useful options

-f   Display images in full-screen mode. (Toggle between full-screen mode and window mode by typing v.)

-s   Display images in a slideshow. (Turn the slideshow on and off by typing s.)

ksnapshot [*options*]   kdegraphics

/usr/bin	stdin	stdout	- file	-- opt	--help	--version

The ksnapshot command is a versatile screen-capture utility. Simply run:

     $ ksnapshot

and it takes a screenshot, displaying it in miniature. From there you can save it to a graphics file or take another screenshot. The only subtlety is choosing a file format for the output; this is done when you save, by choosing an output filename with an appropriate, standard extension: *.jpg* to produce a JPEG file, *.bmp* for a Windows bitmap, *.pbm* for a portable bitmap, *.eps* for encapsulated Postscript, *.ico* for a Windows icon, and so forth. For a list of supported file formats, click the Save Snapshot button and view the selections under Filter.

For more information, click the Help button in the ksnapshot window, or run ksnapshot --help-all from the shell.

gimp [*options*] [*files*]   gimp

/usr/bin	stdin	stdout	- file	-- opt	--help	--version

The GIMP (GNU Image Manipulation Program) is a full-featured image-editing package that rivals Adobe Photoshop in power and scope. It is fairly complex to use but the results can be stunning. Visit *http://www.gimp.org* for full information. To run the program, type:

     $ gimp

To edit a particular file, type:

     $ gimp *filename*

If the GIMP is more complicated than you need, download the xv program for simpler edits, from *http://www.trilon.com/xv*. Simply display the graphics file:

     $ xv myfile.jpg

and click the right mouse button on the image. A menu of editing tools appears.

gnuplot [*options*] [*files*]
gnuplot

/usr/bin	stdin	stdout	- file	-- opt	--help	--version

The gnuplot program creates graphs, plotting points and connecting them with lines and curves, and saves them in a wide variety of printer and plotter formats, such as Postscript. To use gnuplot, you need to learn a small but powerful programming language. Here's an example of plotting the curve $y = x^2$ from $x = 1$ to 10, which will appear in an X window on your display:

```
$ gnuplot
gnuplot> plot [1:10] x**2
gnuplot> quit
```

To do the same, saving the results as a Postscript file:

```
$ echo 'set terminal postscript; plot [1:10] x**2' |
gnuplot > output.ps
```

See *http://www.gnuplot.info* for full details.

xscreensaver
xscreensaver

/usr/X11R6/bin	stdin	stdout	- file	-- opt	**--help**	--version

The xscreensaver system is a versatile screen saver with hundreds of animations available. It runs in the background, and you can control it in various ways:

After a period of inactivity. By default, Fedora's graphical user interfaces (KDE or GNOME) run xscreensaver automatically after five minutes of inactivity. You can configure this from the main menu. In KDE, run the Control Center application, then choose Appearance & Themes, then Screen Saver. Alternatively, right-click your mouse on the desktop, choose Configure Desktop, then choose Screen Saver. In GNOME, choose Preferences/Screensaver from the main menu.

As a screen locker. At any time (in GNOME or KDE), open the main menu and choose Lock Screen. Your display will remain locked until you enter your login password.

On the command line. Run xscreensaver-demo to preview the many animations and set things up the way you like. Then run xscreensaver-command to control the program's behavior:

```
$ xscreensaver-command -activate    Blank now
$ xscreensaver-command -next         Choose next animation
$ xscreensaver-command -prev         Choose previous animation
$ xscreensaver-command -cycle        Choose random animation
$ xscreensaver-command -lock         Lock the screen now
$ xscreensaver-command -exit         Quit
```

Audio and Video

grip	CD player, ripper, and MP3 encoder
xmms	Audio file player (MP3, WAV)
cdparanoia	Rip audio from CDs to WAV files
audacity	Edit audio files
xcdroast	CD burner with graphical interface

Audio is alive and well on Linux systems. Most of the programs we'll cover have intuitive user interfaces, tons of features, and reasonable documentation, so we won't discuss them in detail. Mainly, we want you to have a taste of what's available and possible. Some comprehensive web sites devoted to Linux audio and MIDI are *http://linux-sound.org/* and *http://www.xdt.com/ar/linux-snd*.

Fedora does not include any video players but you can download and install them. Some popular ones are mpg123 (*http://www.mpg123.de/*), smpeg (*http://www.lokigames.com/development/*), and mplayer (*http://www.mplayerhq.hu*).

grip [*options*]   grip

/usr/bin	stdin	stdout	- file	-- opt	--help	--version

grip is a CD player and an audio ripper: it can play CDs, extract audio from CDs, save it in WAV files, and convert the files to MP3s. It has extensive built-in help and fairly intuitive controls.

cdparanoia [*options*] *span* [*outfile*]

/usr/bin   stdin   stdout   - file   -- opt   --help   --version

The cdparanoia command reads (rips) audio data from a CD and stores it in WAV files (or other formats: see the manpage). Common uses are:

$ cdparanoia *N*
> Rip track *N* to a file.

$ cdparanoia -B
> Rip all tracks on the CD into separate files.

$ cdparanoia -B 2-4
> Rip tracks 2, 3, and 4 into separate files.

$ cdparanoia 2-4
> Rip tracks 2, 3, and 4 into a single file.

If you have difficulty accessing your drive, try running cdparanoia -Qvs ("search for CD-ROM drives verbosely") and look for clues. To convert your WAV files to MP3 format, check out LAME (*http://lame.sourceforge.net/*) or NotLame (*http://www.idiap.ch/ ~sanders/not_lame/*).

xmms [*options*] [*files*]

/usr/bin   stdin   stdout   - file   -- opt   --help   --version

xmms (X MultiMedia System) is an excellent, graphical audio-file player that supports MP3, WAV, Ogg Vorbis, and other audio formats.* You can play files with familiar CD-player controls, create playlists, and more. The easiest way to get started is to try it, either with no arguments:

$ xmms

or providing audio files on the command line:

$ xmms file1.mp3 file2.wav file3.ogg ...

Here are some useful actions.

Action	Meaning
Right-click on titlebar	Display main menu
Click PL button	Display playlist (click Add to add files)

* Fedora includes xmms without MP3 support; visit *http://www.xmms.org/* to restore it or to install the latest, untainted version.

Action	Meaning
Click EQ button	Display graphic equalizer
Double-click track in playlist	Play track
Right-click on playlist	Display playlist menu

audacity [*files*]

audacity

not included in Fedora	stdin	stdout	- file	-- opt	--help	--version

audacity is a graphical audio file editor for making changes to WAV, MP3, and Ogg files. Once a file is loaded, you can view its waveform, cut and paste audio data, apply filters and special effects to the sound (echo, bass boost, reverse, etc.), and more. Audacity is not included with Fedora, but it's a highly recommended download from *http://audacity.sourceforge.net*.

xcdroast [*options*]

xcdroast

/usr/bin	stdin	stdout	- file	-- opt	--help	--version

xcdroast is a CD burning program with a graphical user interface. It supports only SCSI CD drives. If your CD writer is an IDE drive, you'll need to configure it to use the *ide-scsi* emulation module. This task is far beyond the scope of our little book, but basically, if your CD drives show up in the output of:

```
$ cdrecord -scanbus
```

you should be OK. Otherwise, consult the "CD-Writing Howto" at *http://www.tldp.org/HOWTO/CD-Writing-HOWTO.html*. Additionally, before using xcdroast, visit *http://www.xcdroast.org* and read the documentation, especially the FAQ, because setup can be tricky. Then run:

```
$ xcdroast
```

Click Setup and make sure all your settings are as you want them. Click Save Configuration, then OK to return to the main screen. From there, choose Duplicate CD or Create CD, whichever you want, and continue from there. Depending on how your system is configured, you might need to be the superuser to burn CDs.

Programming with Shell Scripts

Earlier when we covered the shell (bash), we said it had a programming language built in. In fact, you can write programs, or *shell scripts*, to accomplish tasks that a single command cannot. Like any good programming language, the shell has variables, conditionals (if-then-else), loops, input and output, and more. Entire books have been written on shell scripting, so we'll be covering the bare minimum to get you started. For full documentation, run info bash.

Whitespace and Linebreaks

bash shell scripts are very sensitive to whitespace and linebreaks. Because the "keywords" of this programming language are actually commands evaluated by the shell, you need to separate arguments with whitespace. Likewise, a linebreak in the middle of a command will mislead the shell into thinking the command is incomplete. Follow the conventions we present here and you should be fine.

Variables

We described variables earlier:

```
$ MYVAR=6
$ echo $MYVAR
6
```

All values held in variables are strings, but if they are numeric the shell will treat them as numbers when appropriate.

```
$ NUMBER="10"
$ expr $NUMBER + 5
15
```

When you refer to a variable's value in a shell script, it's a good idea to surround it with double quotes to prevent certain runtime errors. An undefined variable, or a variable with spaces in its value, will evaluate to something unexpected if not surrounded by quotes, causing your script to malfunction.

```
$ FILENAME="My Document"          Space in the name
$ ls $FILENAME                    Try to list it
```

```
ls: My: No such file or directory          Oops! ls saw 2 arguments
ls: Document: No such file or directory
$ ls -l "$FILENAME"                        List it properly
My Document                                ls saw only 1 argument
```

If a variable name is evaluated adjacent to another string, surround it with curly braces to prevent unexpected behavior:

```
$ HAT="fedora"
$ echo "The plural of $HAT is $HATs"
The plural of fedora is                    Oops! No variable "HATs"
$ echo  "The plural of $HAT is ${HAT}s"
The plural of fedora is fedoras            What we wanted
```

Input and Output

Script output is provided by the echo and printf commands,
which we described in "Screen Output" on page 144:

```
$ echo "Hello world"
Hello world
$ printf "I am %d years old\n" `expr 20 + 20`
I am 40 years old
```

Input is provided by the read command, which reads one line
from standard input and stores it in a variable:

```
$ read name
Sandy Smith <ENTER>
$ echo "I read the name $name"
I read the name Sandy Smith
```

Booleans and Return Codes

Before we can describe conditionals and loops, we need the
concept of a Boolean (true/false) test. To the shell, the value
0 means true or success, and anything else means false or
failure.

Additionally, every Linux command returns an integer value,
called a *return code* or *exit status*, to the shell when the command exits. You can see this value in the special variable $?:

```
$ cat myfile
My name is Sandy Smith and
```

```
I really like Fedora Linux
$ grep Smith myfile
My name is Sandy Smith and          A match was found...
$ echo $?
0                                   ...so return code is "success"
$ grep aardvark myfile
$ echo $?                           No match was found...
1                                   ...so return code is "failure"
```

The return codes of a command are usually documented on its manpage.

test and "["

The test command (built into the shell) will evaluate simple Boolean expressions involving numbers and strings, setting its exit status to 0 (true) or 1 (false):

```
$ test 10 -lt 5       Is 10 less than 5?
$ echo $?
1                     No, it isn't
$ test -n "hello"     Does the string "hello" have nonzero length?
$ echo $?
0                     Yes, it does
```

A list of common test arguments are found in Table 12, for checking properties of integers, strings, and files.

test has an unusual alias, "[" (left square bracket), as a shorthand for use with conditionals and loops. If you use this shorthand, you must supply a final argument of "]" (right square bracket) to signify the end of the test. The following tests are identical to those before:

```
$ [ 10 -lt 5 ]
$ echo $?
1
$ [ -n "hello" ]
$ echo $?
0
```

Remember that "[" is a command like any other, so it is followed by *individual arguments separated by whitespace*. So if you mistakenly forget some whitespace:

```
$ [ 5 -lt 4]          No space between 4 and ]
bash: [: missing ']'
```

then test thinks the final argument is the string "4]" and complains that the final bracket is missing.

Table 12. Some common arguments for the test command

File tests	
-d *name*	File *name* is a directory
-f *name*	File *name* is a regular file
-L *name*	File *name* is a symbolic link
-r *name*	File *name* exists and is readable
-w *name*	File *name* exists and is writable
-x *name*	File *name* exists and is executable
-s *name*	File *name* exists and its size is nonzero
f1 -nt *f2*	File *f1* is newer than file *f2*
f1 -ot *f2*	File *f1* is older than file *f2*
String tests	
s1 = *s2*	String *s1* equals string *s2*
s1 != *s2*	String *s1* does not equal string *s2*
-z *s1*	String *s1* has zero length
-n *s1*	String *s1* has nonzero length
Numeric tests	
a -eq *b*	Integers *a* and *b* are equal
a -ne *b*	Integers *a* and *b* are not equal
a -gt *b*	Integer *a* is greater than integer *b*
a -ge *b*	Integer *a* is greater than or equal to integer *b*
a -lt *b*	Integer *a* is less than integer *b*
a -le *b*	Integer *a* is less than or equal to integer *b*
Combining and negating tests	
t1 -a t1	And: Both tests t1 and t2 are true
t1 -o t2	Or: Either test t1 or t2 is true
! *your_test*	Negate the test, i.e., your_test is false
\(*your_test* \)	Parentheses are used for grouping, as in algebra

true and false

bash has built-in commands true and false, which simply set
their exit status to 0 and 1, respectively.

```
$ true
$ echo $?
0
$ false
$ echo $?
1
```

These will be useful when we discuss conditionals and loops.

Conditionals

The if statement chooses between alternatives, each of which
may have a complex test. The simplest form is the if-then
statement:

```
if command            If exit status of command is 0
then
  body
fi
```

For example:

```
if [ `whoami` = "root" ]
then
  echo "You are the superuser"
fi
```

Next is the if-then-else statement:

```
if command
then
  body1
else
  body2
fi
```

For example:

```
if [ `whoami` = "root" ]
then
  echo "You are the superuser"
else
  echo "You are an ordinary dude"
fi
```

Finally, we have the form if-then-elif-else, which may have as many tests as you like:

```
if command1
then
   body1
elif command2
then
   body2
elif ...
   ...
else
   bodyN
fi
```

For example:

```
if [ `whoami` = "root" ]
then
   echo "You are the superuser"
elif [ "$USER" = "root" ]
then
   echo "You might be the superuser"
elif [ "$bribe" -gt 10000 ]
then
   echo "You can pay to be the superuser"
else
   echo "You are still an ordinary dude"
fi
```

The case statement evaluates a single value and branches to an appropriate piece of code:

```
echo 'What would you like to do?'
read answer
case "$answer" in
  eat)
    echo "OK, have a hamburger"
    ;;
  sleep)
    echo "Good night then"
    ;;
  *)
    echo "I'm not sure what you want to do"
    echo "I guess I'll see you tomorrow"
    ;;
esac
```

The general form is:

```
case string in
  expr1)
    body1
    ;;
  expr2)
    body2
    ;;
  ...
  exprN)
    bodyN
    ;;
  *)
    bodyelse
    ;;
esac
```

where *string* is any value, usually a variable value like
$myvar, and *expr1* through *exprN* are patterns (run the com-
mand info bash reserved case for details), with the final *
like a final "else." Each set of commands must be terminated
by ;; (as shown):

```
case $letter in
  X)
    echo "$letter is an X"
    ;;
  [aeiou])
    echo "$letter is a vowel"
    ;;
  [0-9])
    echo "$letter is a digit, silly"
    ;;
  *)
    echo "I cannot handle that"
    ;;
esac
```

Loops

The while loop repeats a set of commands as long as a condition is true.

```
while command              While the exit status of command is 0
do
  body
done
```

For example, if this is the script myscript:

```
i=0
while [ $i -lt 3 ]
do
  echo "again"
  i=`expr $i + 1`
done

$ ./myscript
0
1
2
```

The until loop repeats until a condition becomes true:

```
until command              While the exit status of command is nonzero
do
  body
done
```

For example:

```
i=0
until [ $i -gt 3 ]
do
  echo "again"
  i=`expr $i + 1`
done

$ ./myscript
0
1
2
```

The for loop iterates over values from a list:

```
for variable in list
do
  body
done
```

For example:

```
for name in Tom Jack Harry
do
  echo "$name is my friend"
done
```

```
$ ./myscript
Tom is my friend
Jack is my friend
Harry is my friend
```

The for loop is particularly handy for processing lists of files, for example, all files of a certain type in the current directory:

```
for file in *.doc
do
  echo "$file is a stinky Microsoft Word file"
done
```

For an infinite loop, use while with the condition true, or until with the condition false:

```
while true
do
  echo "forever"
done

until false
do
  echo "forever again"
done
```

Presumably you would use break or exit to terminate these loops based on some condition.

Break and Continue

The break command jumps out of the nearest enclosing loop. Consider this simple script called myscript:

```
for name in Tom Jack Harry
do
  echo $name
  echo "again"
done
echo "all done"

$ ./myscript
Tom
again
Jack
again
```

```
Harry
again
all done
```

Now with a break:

```
for name in Tom Jack Harry
do
  echo $name
  if [ "$name" = "Jack" ]
  then
    break
  fi
  echo "again"
done
echo "all done"

$ ./myscript
Tom
again
Jack            The break occurs
all done
```

The continue command forces a loop to jump to its next iteration.

```
for name in Tom Jack Harry
do
  echo $name
  if [ "$name" = "Jack" ]
  then
    continue
  fi
  echo "again"
done
echo "all done"

$ ./myscript
Tom
again
Jack            The continue occurs
Harry
again
all done
```

break and continue also accept a numeric argument (break N, continue N) to control multiple layers of loops (e.g., jump out of *N* layers of loops), but this kind of scripting leads to spaghetti code and we don't recommend it.

Creating and Running Shell Scripts

To create a shell script, simply put bash commands into a file as you would type them. To run the script, you have three choices:

Prepend #!/bin/bash and make the file executable
>   This is the most common way to run scripts. Add the line:

>   #!/bin/bash

>   to the very top of the script file. It must be the first line of the file, left-justified. Then make the file executable:

> $ chmod +x myscript

>   Optionally, move it into a directory in your search path. Then run it like any other command:

> $ myscript

>   If the script is in your current directory, but the current directory "." is not in your search path, you'll need to prepend "./" so the shell finds the script:

> $ ./myscript

>   The current directory is generally not in your search path for security reasons.

Pass to bash
>   bash will interpret its argument as the name of a script and run it.

> $ bash myscript

Run in current shell with "."
>   The preceding methods run your script as an independent entity that has no effect on your current shell.[*] If you want your script to make changes to your current

---

[*] Technically, it runs in a separate shell (a *subshell* or *child shell*) that inherits the attributes of the original shell, but cannot alter them in the original shell.

shell (setting variables, changing directory, and so on), it can be run in the current shell with the "." command:

```
$ . myscript
```

Command-Line Arguments

Shell scripts can accept command-line arguments and options just like other Linux commands. (In fact, some common Linux commands *are* scripts.) Within your shell script, you can refer to these arguments as $1, $2, $3, and so on.

```
$ cat myscript
#!/bin/bash
echo "My name is $1 and I come from $2"

$ ./myscript Johnson Wisconsin
My name is Johnson and I come from Wisconsin
$ ./myscript Bob
My name is Bob and I come from
```

Your script can test the number of arguments it received with $#:

```
if [ $# -lt 2 ]
then
  echo "$0 error: you must supply two arguments"
else
  echo "My name is $1 and I come from $2"
fi
```

The special value $0 contains the name of the script, and is handy for usage and error messages:

```
$ ./myscript Bob
./myscript error: you must supply two arguments
```

To iterate over all command-line arguments, use a for loop with the special variable $@, which holds all arguments:

```
for arg in $@
do
  echo "I found the argument $arg"
done
```

Exiting with a Return Code

The exit command terminates your script and passes a given return code to the shell. By tradition, scripts should return 0 for success and 1 (or other nonzero value) on failure. If your script doesn't call exit, the return code is automatically 0.

```
if [ $# -lt 2 ]
then
  echo "Error: you must supply two arguments"
  exit 1
else
  echo "My name is $1 and I come from $2"
fi
exit 0

$ ./myscript Bob
./myscript error: you must supply two arguments
$ echo $?
1
```

Beyond Shell Scripting

Shell scripts are fine for many purposes, but Linux comes with much more powerful scripting languages, as well as compiled programming languages. Here are a few.

Language	Program	To get started...
Perl	perl	man perl *http://www.perl.com/*
Python	python	man python *http://www.python.org/*
C, C++	gcc	man gcc *http://www.gnu.org/software/gcc/*
Java	javac[a]	*http://java.sun.com/*
FORTRAN	g77	man g77 *http://www.gnu.org/software/fortran/fortran.html*
Ada	gnat	info gnat *http://www.gnu.org/software/gnat/gnat.html*

[a] Not included in Fedora, nor many other Linux distros.

Final Words

Although we've covered many commands and capabilities of Linux, we've just scratched the surface. Fedora and other distributions come with *thousands* of other programs. We encourage you to continue reading, exploring, and learning the capabilities of your Linux systems. Good luck!

Acknowledgments

Heartfelt thanks to my editor Mike Loukides, the O'Reilly production staff, the technical reviewers (Ron Bellomo, Wesley Crossman, David Debonnaire, Tim Greer, Jacob Heider, and Eric van Oorschot), Alex Schowtka and Robert Dulaney at VistaPrint, and my wonderful family, Lisa and Sophie.

Index

Symbols

!! (recalling previous
    command), 29
/ (slash), root directory, 13
& (ampersand), running
    background jobs, 30
&& (two ampersands), stopping
    execution of combined
    commands, 27
. (period), current directory, 14
.. (two periods), parent
    directory, 14
; (semicolon), combine
    commands using, 26
[(left square bracket), alias for
    test command, 168
\ (forward slash), escaping
    special characters, 27
^Z command (suspending
    jobs), 31
| (pipe operator), 26
||, stopping execution of
    combined commands, 27
~ (tilde), denoting home
    directories, 15, 23

A

abiword program, 56
absolute path of current
    directory, printing, 41
acroread viewer, 49
Ada language, 178
alias command, 25
alphabetical order, sorting text
    in, 77
ampersand (&), running
    background jobs, 30
apt program, 35
arguments for commands, 3
aspell command, 103
at command, 156–157
atq command, 157
atrm command, 157
attributes of files
    changing, 64
    viewing, 65
audacity graphical audio file
    editor, 165
audio on Linux
    systems, 163–165
awk filter program, 81
    vs. tr command, 77

We'd like to hear your suggestions for improving our indexes. Send email to
index@oreilly.com.

B

background jobs, running, 30
backing up Linux files, 95–101
backquotes on command line, 27
basename command, 42
bash (Bourne Again Shell), 2, 20–33
  command-line editing, 28
  printf command, 146
  programming with shell scripts, 166–176
  type command, 66, 70
bg command, 31
  jobs command and, 30
bin directory, 16
Booleans in shell scripts, 167, 170
/boot directory, 18
Bourne Again Shell (see bash)
brace expansion, 23
break command, 174
browsing the web, 136–140
bunzip2 command, 84
burning CDs, 99, 165
bzcat command, 84
bzip2 command, 84
  tar –j command and, 99

C

C and C++ languages, 178
^C command (killing programs), 32
cal command, 153
Calc program (soffice), 56
calculator command (dc), 151
calculator programs, 149–152
case statement, 171
cat command, 43
  tee command and, 80
CD burning programs, 99, 165

cd command, 14, 41
  home directories, locating, 14
cdparanoia command, 164
cdrecord command, 99
  xcdroast command and, 165
cgi-bin directory, 16
chattr (change attributes) command, 64
checksums, comparing, 90
chfn (change finger) command, 117
chgrp command, 20, 62, 120
chmod command, 20, 62–64
chown command, 20, 61
chsh (change shell) command, 118
cksum program, 86, 90
clear command, 149
clock programs, 152
cmp command, 86, 89
columns of text, extracting from files, 75
combining commands, 26
comm command, 86, 88
command-line arguments in shell scripts, 177
command-line editing with bash, 28
commands, 3
  combining, 26
  history-related, 29
  killing, 32, 109
comparing files, 86–90
completing filenames with TAB key, 29
compress command, 83
  software installation and, 34
  tar –Z command and, 99
  zip command and, 85
compressing/uncompressing files, 82–85

conditionals in shell
    scripts, 170–172
configure script, running, 37
configuring the shell, 33
connecting to
    networks, 128–131
continue command, 175
controlling processes, 108–110
cp command, 39
cpio program, 96
cron process, 158
crontab command, 158–159
CUPS printing system, 101
curl command, 138
curly-brace expressions,
    expanding, 23
cut command, 75

D

date command, 153–155
    watch command and, 156
dc (desk calculator)
    command, 151
dd program, 96
default editor, setting, 52
dev directory, 17
df (disk free) program, 92
diff program, 86
diff3 program, 86, 88
dig command, 125
directories, Linux, 13
    changing, using cd
        command, 41
    creating, 42
    deleting empty directories, 42
    home directories, 14
    operating system
        directories, 18
    printing absolute path of, 41
    system directories, 15–18
dirname command, 42

disk usage command (du), 59
disks and filesystems, 91–95
DISPLAY variable, 23
dnsdomainname command, 121
doc directory, 16
domainname command, 121
du (disk usage) command, 59
dump command, 96
    chattr command and, 64
    restore command and, 97
DVI files, 50
dvips command, 50

E

echo command, 7, 145
    script output provided
        by, 167
ed line editor, 81
    diff –e command, 87
EDITOR environment
    variable, 45
    setting default editor, 52
egrep command, 73
else statement, 170
emacs text editor
    command-line editing, 28
    creating/editing files, 51–54
    lynx –emacskeys
        command, 138
    RPM filenames and, 35
email readers, 132–135
environment variables, 24
    EDITOR, 45, 52
    HOME, 15, 23
    preserving, in new shell, 119
    printing, 114
    VISUAL, 45, 52
eog (Eye of Gnome) image
    viewer, 160
Epiphany web browser for
    GNOME, 136

escaping special characters, 27
etc directory, 16
evolution command, 132
Excel documents
    editing with abiword, 56
    editing with soffice, 55
exit command, 12
    exiting with return codes, 178
    terminating loops, 174
    terminating shells, 33
exit status (return codes) of
        Linux commands, 167
export command, 24
expr command, 149
ext3 filesystems, 91
    chattr/lsattr commands, 64
Eye of Gnome (eog) image
        viewer, 160

F

false command, 170
    infinite loops and, 174
fdisk program, 95
Fedora Linux, 2
    getting help with, 8
    graphical desktop, 9
    running shell windows, 11
    up2date command, 34
fg command, 32
    jobs command and, 30
fgrep command, 74
file command, 59
filename completion, 29
files
    changing timestamps, 60
    copying, using cp
        command, 39
    creating, 51–56
    deleting, using rm
        command, 39
    editing, 51–56

linking, using ln
        command, 40
    listing attributes of, 57
    listing, using ls command, 38
    locating, 65–71
    measuring disk space of, 59
    moving, 39
    permissions/ownership, 19,
        38, 62–64
    renaming, 39
    setting group ownership
        of, 62
    setting ownership of, 61
    viewing, 43–51
    word count program, 58
filesystem, Linux, 13–20
find command, 66–68
finger command, 113, 117
Firebird web browser, 136
floppy program, 95
fonts directory, 16
for loops, 173
    command-line arguments
        and, 177
foreground, bringing jobs
        into, 32
formatting disks, 91, 95
FORTRAN language, 178
forward slash (\), escaping
        special characters, 27
free command, 108
fsck command, 94
    shutdown command and, 12
ftp (File Transfer Protocol)
        program, 131

G

g77 program, 178
gaim program, 142
Galeon web browser, 136
gcc program, 178

ghostview command, 49
  DVI files and, 50
GIMP (GNU Image
      Manipulation
      Program), 161
gnat program, 178
GNOME graphical
      environment, 2
  Epiphany web browser, 136
  Fedora Linux and, 10
  getting help with, 8
  logging out/shutting
      down, 11
  running shells within, 11
  xclock command, 152
  xscreensaver program, 162
gnome-terminal program, 11
gnumeric program, 56
gnuplot program, 162
Google, getting help from, 9
gqview image viewer, 160
graphical desktop, 9
graphics, viewing/
      editing, 160–163
grep command, 71
  egrep command and, 73
  fgrep command and, 74
  manipulating RPM
      packages, 35
  ps command and, 105
grip command, 163
groupadd command, 120
groupdel command, 120
groupmod command, 121
groups command, 119
  id –Gn command and, 112
gunzip command, 83
gv command, 49
  DVI files and, 50
gzip command, 83
  software installation and, 34
  tar –z command and, 99

H

hard links, 40
head command, 45
help and tutorials, 7
--help option, 8
hexadecimal dump of binary
      files, 48
history command, 29
home directories, 14
HOME environment
      variable, 15, 23
host command, 124
hostname command, 122
html directory, 16

I

id command, 112
if statement, 170
ifconfig command, 123
if-then-elif-else statement, 171
Impress program (soffice), 56
include directory, 16
index of file locations,
      creating, 69
info command, 8
init.d directory, 16
input in shell scripts, 167
input/output redirection, 26
installing software on the Linux
      system, 33–37
instant messaging on
      Linux, 142–144
Internet domains, looking up
      registration of, 125

J

Java language, 178
javac program, 178
job control in Linux
      shells, 30–32

jobs command, 30
jobs, scheduling, 155–159

K

KDE graphical environment, 2
  Fedora Linux and, 10
  getting help with, 8
  Konquerer web browser, 136
  logging out/shutting
    down, 11
  running shells within, 11
  xclock command, 152
  xscreensaver program, 162
Kerberos
  /usr/kerberos directory, 17
  telnet command and, 129
kill command, 32, 109
Konquerer web browser for
  KDE, 136
konsole program, 11
ksnapshot command, 161

L

last command, 114
less command, 44
  cat command and, 43
lib directory, 16
libexec directory, 16
linebreaks in shell scripts, 166
linking files, 40
Linux
  backing up files, 95–101
  components of, 2
  filesystem, layout of, 13–20
  getting help with, 7
  installing software on the
    system, 33–37
  spell checkers in, 103–104
ln command, 40
lock directory, 17
log directory, 17

logname command, 111
LOGNAME variable, 24
logout command, 12
look command, 103
loops in shell scripts, 172–174
/lost+found directory, 18
lpq (line printer queue)
    command, 102
lpr (line printer) command, 101
lprm (line printer remove)
    command, 102
LPRng printing system, 101
ls command, 6, 38
  displaying file properties, 57
  file protections and, 19
lsattr (list attributes)
    command, 65
lynx command, 136–138

M

m4 macro-processing
    language, 81
magnetic tape command
    (mt), 96
mail directory, 17
mail program, 135
mail readers, 132–135
MAIL variable, 24
mailq command, 132
make command, 37
make install command, 37
man command, 8, 16
man directory, 16
masks and protection modes, 55
math commands, 149–152
md5sum program, 86, 90
memory usage, displaying, 108
mesg program, 113, 144
Microsoft Excel documents
  editing with abiword, 56
  editing with soffice, 55

Microsoft Word documents
    editing with abiword, 56
    editing with soffice, 55
misc directory, 17
mkdir command, 42
mkfs program, 95
mkisofs command, 99
mnt directory, 17
mount command, 93
Mozilla web browser, 136
    reading email, 132
    reading Usenet news, 140
mpg123 video player, 163
mplayer video player, 163
mt (magnetic tape)
        command, 96
mutt mailer, 133–135
mv command, 39

N

Netscape web browser, 136
network connections,
        establishing, 128–131
network interface, displaying
        information about, 123
news, Usenet, 9, 140–142
nice command, 109
nisdomainname command, 121
nl command, 46
    cat command and, 44
nslookup command, 125
ntpdate command, 155

O

oclock program, 152
octal dump (od) command, 47
od (octal dump) command, 47
OLDPWD variable, 24
OpenOffice.org package, 55
Opera web browser, 136

operating system directories, 18
options for commands, 3
output in shell scripts, 167
ownership of files, 19, 38, 62–64

P

parted program, 95
partitioning disks, 91, 95
passwd command, 117
paste command, 75
patch command, 87
PATH variable, 24–25
Perl language, 178
permissions, file, 19, 38, 62–64
pidof command, 109
pine mail program, 132
ping command, 126
pipe (|) operator, 26
printenv command, 114
    at command and, 157
printf command, 146–147
    script output provided
        by, 167
–printf option (find
        command), 68
printing systems in Linux, 101
/proc directory, 17, 18
processes
    controlling, 108–110
    viewing, 104–108
ps command, 104, 109
public_html directory, 16
pwd command, 41
PWD variable, 24
Python language, 178

Q

quoting on command line, 27

R

rc.d directory, 16
rcsdiff program, 87
read command, 167
Red Hat Linux, 3
Red Hat Package Manager
        (RPM) files, 34
redhat-config-printer
        command, 102
redirecting input/output, 26
regular expressions
    awk filter and, 81
    egrep command, 73
    find –regex command, 66
    grep command, 71
    less command and, 44
    slocate –r command, 69
remote machines
    logging into with telnet, 129
    looking up hostnames, 124
    sending ICMP packets to, 126
    traceroute command, 127
renice command, 110
reset command, 33
restore command, 97
    mt command and, 96
resuming jobs with fg
        command, 32
return codes of Linux
        commands, 167, 178
rm command, 39
RMAIL program, 132
rmdir command, 42
root directory (/), 13
root user, 4, 118
RPM (Red Hat Package
        Manager) files, 34
rpm command, 34–36
RPM packages, commands for
        manipulating, 35

S

rsync command, 100
run directory, 17

sbin directory, 16
scalc command, 56
scheduling jobs, 155–159
scp (secure copy)
        command, 130
screensavers
    viewing/editing, 160–163
    xscreensaver program, 162
sdiff program, 86, 88
sdraw command, 56
secure copy (scp)
        command, 130
secure shell (ssh) program, 128
sed filter program, 81
    vs. tr command, 77
semicolon (;), combine
        commands using, 26
sendmail program, 133
seq command, 148
sfax command, 56
sfdisk program, 95
sftp program, 130
share directory, 16
shell prompts, 3
    for superuser commands, 4
shell scripts
    break and continue in, 174
    command-line arguments
        in, 177
    conditionals in, 170–172
    creating, 176
    exiting with return codes, 178
    loops in, 172–174
    programming with, 166–178
    running, 176
SHELL variable, 24

shell windows, opening, 11
shells, 20–33
    changing login shell
        program, 118
    history-related commands, 29
    job control, 30–32
    running, 11
    suspending, 31
    terminating, 33
    vs. programs, 21
    (see also bash)
shutdown command, 12
simpress command, 56
slabel command, 56
slash (/), root directory, 13
sleep command, 156
slocate (secure locate)
        command, 69
    locating files, 66
slrn newsreader, 140–142
smpeg video player, 163
soffice program, 55
sort command, 77
special characters, escaping, 27
spell checkers in Linux, 103–104
spell command, 104
spool directory, 17
src directory, 16
ssh (secure shell) program, 128
standard output, printing
        messages on, 144–149
stat command, 57
su command, 5
    becoming superuser, 118
    software installation and, 34
    whoami command and, 111
subdirectories, Linux, 13
sudo program, 119
sum program, 86, 90
superusers, 4
    becoming, 118

suspend command, 31
swriter command, 56
symbolic links, 40
sync command, 64, 94
system directories, 15–18
system load, displaying
        graphically, 107

T

t3d clock program, 152
TAB key, completing filenames
        with, 29
tail command, 46
talk program, 143
tape drives, copying files to, 96
tar command, 98
    mt command and, 96
    software installation and, 34
tar files, 36
    compressed, sample
        commands, 84, 85
    gzipped, sample
        commands, 83
tee command, 80
telnet program, 129
TERM variable, 24
terminating shells, 33
test command, 168–169
text manipulation
        commands, 71–80
tilde (~), denoting home
        directories, 15, 23
time, displaying/
        setting, 152–155
timestamps, changing, 60
tmp directory, 17
top command, 106
touch command, 60
    creating empty files, 51
tr command, 76
traceroute command, 127

translating characters, using tr
        command, 76
true command, 170
    infinite loops and, 174
tty program, 144
tutorials
    for emacs, 52
    getting help with Linux, 7
    for mutt mailer, 135
    for vim editor, 53
twm graphical environment, 10
    running shells within, 11
type command, 66, 70
    locating files, 66
types of files, reporting, 59

U

umask command, 54
umount command, 93
uname command, 19, 122
uncompress command, 83
uniq command, 79
until loops, 173
    infinite loops and, 174
unzip command, 85
up2date command, 34
uptime command, 19, 105
Usenet news, 9, 140–142
USER variable, 24
useradd command, 115
userdel command, 116
usermod command, 116
users
    creating new accounts, 115
    deleting existing users, 116
    finger command and, 113
    listing logged-in users, 112
    modifying accounts, 116
    printenv command and, 114
    printing login names, 111

    printing user IDs, 112
    superusers and, 4
    updating information, 117
users command, 113
/usr/share/doc directory, 8
uudecode command, 85
uuencode command, 85
uxterm program, 11

V

var directory, 17
variables
    defining, 23
    in shell scripts, 166
vfat filesystems, 91
vi text editor, 51
    command-line editing, 28
    less command, 45
    lynx –vikeys command, 138
video on Linux systems, 163
viewing
    files, 43–51
    processes, 104–108
vim text editor, 51, 53
    lynx –vikeys command, 138
    sed filter and, 81
VISUAL environment
        variable, 45
    setting default editor, 52

W

w command, 106
watch command, 156
wc command, 3, 58
web browsing, 136–140
wget command, 138–140
whereis command, 70
    locating files, 66
which command, 70
    locating files, 66

while loops, 172
  infinite loops and, 174
whitespace
  programming with shell
       scripts, 166
  quoting on command line, 27
who command, 112
  tee command and, 80
whoami command, 111
whois command, 125
wildcard characters and the
       shell, 22
windows (shell), opening, 11
Word documents
  editing with abiword, 56
  editing with soffice, 55
write program, 143
Writer program (soffice), 56
www directory, 16

X

X11 directory, 17
xargs command, 68
xcalc command, 149
xcdroast program, 100, 165
xclock command, 152
xdvi command, 50

Ximian Evolution program, 132
xload command, 107
xmms command, 164
xpdf viewer, 49
xscreensaver program, 162
xscreensaver-command
       command, 163
xscreensaver-demo
       command, 163
xterm program, 11
xv program, using instead of
       GIMP, 161
xxd command, 48
xxdiff program, 86

Y

yes command, 147
ypdomainname command, 121
yum program, 35

Z

^Z command (suspending
       jobs), 31
zcat command, 83
zip command, 85

Related Titles Available from O'Reilly

Linux

O'REILLY®

Keep in touch with O'Reilly

1. Download examples from our books

To find example files for a book, go to:
> *www.oreilly.com/catalog*

select the book, and follow the "Examples" link.

2. Register your O'Reilly books

Register your book at *register.oreilly.com*

Why register your books? Once you've registered your O'Reilly books you can:

* Win O'Reilly books, T-shirts or discount coupons in our monthly drawing.
* Get special offers available only to registered O'Reilly customers.
* Get catalogs announcing new books (US and UK only).
* Get email notification of new editions of the O'Reilly books you own.

3. Join our email lists

Sign up to get topic-specific email announcements of new books and conferences, special offers, and O'Reilly Network technology newsletters at:
> *elists.oreilly.com*

It's easy to customize your free elists subscription so you'll get exactly the O'Reilly news you want.

4. Get the latest news, tips, and tools
> *www.oreilly.com*

* "Top 100 Sites on the Web"—PC Magazine
* CIO Magazine's Web Business 50 Awards

Our web site contains a library of comprehensive product information (including book excerpts and tables of contents), downloadable software, background articles, interviews with technology leaders, links to relevant sites, book cover art, and more.

5. Work for O'Reilly

Check out our web site for current employment opportunities:
> *jobs.oreilly.com*

6. Contact us

O'Reilly & Associates
1005 Gravenstein Hwy North
Sebastopol, CA 95472 USA

TEL: 707-827-7000 or 800-998-9938
      (6am to 5pm PST)

FAX: 707-829-0104

order@oreilly.com
> For answers to problems regarding your order or our products.
> To place a book order online, visit:
> *www.oreilly.com/order_new*

catalog@oreilly.com
> To request a copy of our latest catalog.

booktech@oreilly.com
> For book content technical questions or corrections.

corporate@oreilly.com
> For educational, library, government, and corporate sales.

proposals@oreilly.com
> To submit new book proposals to our editors and product managers.

international@oreilly.com
> For information about our international distributors or translation queries. For a list of our distributors outside of North America check out:
> *international.oreilly.com/distributors.html*

adoption@oreilly.com
> For information about academic use of O'Reilly books, visit:
> *academic.oreilly.com*

O'REILLY®

Our books are available at most retail and online bookstores.
To order direct: 1-800-998-9938 • *order@oreilly.com* • *www.oreilly.com*
Online editions of most O'Reilly titles are available at *safari.oreilly.com*